Idol™Icon

Idol ᵀᴼ Icon

The creation of celebrity brands

Gerrie Lim

Copyright © 2005 Gerrie Lim

First published in 2005 by:

Marshall Cavendish Business
An imprint of Marshall Cavendish International (Asia) Private Limited
A member of Times Publishing Limited
Times Centre, 1 New Industrial Road
Singapore 536196
T: +65 6213 9300
F: +65 6285 4871
E: te@sg.marshallcavendish.com
Online bookstore: www.marshallcavendish.com/genref

and

Cyan Communications Limited
4.3 The Ziggurat
60–66 Saffron Hill
London EC1N 8QX
United Kingdom
www.cyanbooks.com

A CIP record for this book is available from the British Library

ISBN 981 261 801 5 (Asia & ANZ)
ISBN 1-904879-18-7 (Rest of world)

Designed and typeset by Curran Publishing Services, Norwich, UK

Printed and bound in Singapore

For P. H.
"Brad who?"

"I look at what I design and I think, 'Is this cool? Would Keith Richards or Anita Pallenberg wear these clothes?'"

Anna Sui, fashion designer

"To succeed and then achieve longevity, she knew she had to embrace the nature and power of image. Styling, make-up and hair combine to create a persona and can embellish and extend the personality of the performer.... Image can provide a mask, concealing true nature and creating a perfected and fantastic illusion."

William Baker, celebrity stylist, on his client Kylie Minogue

CONTENTS

INTERVIEWS

PREFACE

Just Push Play (But a Word of Warning)

The genesis of this book can be traced back to December 2001, when I interviewed the advertising mogul Ian Batey for an article on branding for the now-defunct magazine *Business Online*. Ian was then promoting his new book, *Asian Branding*, and we had a very enjoyable chat, made easier by the fact that we already knew one another – I had previously worked for him. In 1989 and 1990 I was a copywriter at his Singapore agency, Batey Ads, whose crowning glories were the many award-winning Singapore Airlines campaigns bearing the ubiquitous slogan, "Singapore Girl, you're a great way to fly."

That article I wrote, "Building Asia's Killer Brands," made mention of how only five Asian brands (Honda, Nintendo, Samsung, Sony, and Toyota), appeared in Interbrand's 2001 list of the world's top 50 brands. This, along with the "Singapore Girl" notion, made me think of the marketing concept of "singularity": how product differentiation is created by placing focus on unique characteristics. It also took me back to the start of that year; I had begun 2001 by meeting and interviewing the actress/singer/nascent-superstar Jennifer Lopez for a California newspaper, the *San Diego Union-Tribune*. There was a full circle, a coming together of sorts.

And so in 2004 I found myself extending my own long-time interest in pop culture by combining it with my new-found interest in branding, resulting in this book. However, this is not a traditional book for the business-book reader, nor is it easy fodder for fans of the pop press. It is not a book about those traditional modes defined (or rather confined) by product/service/corporate branding. Celebrity branding is much more difficult to frame and contain in any single branding theory.

My trusty *Webster's* defines a celebrity as "a famous person," and a brand as "a mark made by a hot iron ... to identify ownership" or "an identification mark, a proprietary make, blend, etc.," as in "a brand of tea." As modern branding expert Tom Blackett points out in his article "What is a Brand?" (2003), the word "brand" actually comes from the Old Norse language – "brandr," meaning "to burn" – and this then somehow crept into Anglo-Saxon usage.

What I am attempting to address is the ever-exciting confluence of celebrities and branding, how certain people have made their own hot mark with the metaphorical iron. But the reader would do well to note that since this is not a typical business or management book, popular buzzwords like "brand development" and "brand management" are not used. Astute readers will realize that I am constantly talking about enhancing personal "brand equity" – but without ever calling it such.

Why? Because we are entering uncharted waters, and the field is so new that to my mind any definitive attempt at defining terms or claiming parameters would be premature and even pretentious. You are instead invited to come on a journey where no easy answers can be found, where the intersection of celebrity and branding only conjures images and emotions resulting in more questions, or at best partial answers.

As such, the actual reading becomes an interactive adventure. Those unused to the first-person format of "New journalism," along the lines of writers like Joan Didion (on whom I wrote my Master's thesis, in fact), may find this rather difficult. Readers used to "how-to" tomes aimed at "leveraging untapped marketing potential" may be sorely disappointed. This book doesn't tell you how to do anything, except perhaps how to think about celebrity in fresh new ways.

A case in point: Peter Fonda and Dennis Hopper surely did wonders for Harley-Davidson's branding, thanks to their appearance in the classic biker film *Easy Rider*, but it's nigh-high impossible to quantify how much they contributed to the current US$7.1 billion worth of the company itself (according to a *Business Week* study). This book is a long meditation on the value of such intangibles, but doesn't provide the magic formula. Unlike traditional product branding, there is no single master plan. This book, then, is an exercise in the mental sport of Zen archery, where nobody can tell you how to hit the target, only that you must. Read it as such, and much pleasure awaits.

I would like to extend my thanks to Martin Liu and Linette Tye at Cyan Books for their ongoing enthusiasm, Pom Somkabcharti for overseeing production, Susan Curran for her meticulous copy-editing, and Adrian Weston for spearheading publicity. Also, special thanks to Christopher Newson, David Yip, and Tan Joo Sin at Marshall Cavendish International Asia in Singapore.

I am grateful to the following people who contributed their insight: Linda Bladholm, Kelly Chew, Bill Clark, Kim-Van Dang, Hans Ebert, Ben Harrison, Jamie Klingler, Ronnie Lippin, Stuart Lloyd, Mohan Mahapatra, Jordan Raphael, Gary See, Bill Wasserzieher, Russel Wong, Eric Yeo, and Kieven Yim. I would also like to thank my own branding consultant: Richard Loh, CEO of The Ploh Group (*www.plohdirect.com*), for reading some chapters and offering suggestions.

I owe an incalculable debt to my friend and beer buddy Kevin Reagan, who declined to participate in this book despite his brilliant track record (as Madonna's art director, he won two Grammy awards for his CD packaging for her *Ray of Light* and *Music* albums), for the many talks we've had in the past about pop stars and their place in the universe. Kevin and I first met because of an Aerosmith album package that he designed, *Just Push Play*, a title rife with irony and sheer inspiration in itself.

Finally, as always, thanks to P. H., particularly for her understanding during those months in mid-2004 when I was finishing this book and desperately trying not to lose my mind, which we both agree would be such a terrible thing to waste.

Gerrie Lim

1
Introduction: In Praise of Idle Worship

When I met Jennifer Lopez in January 2001, in her suite at the Four Seasons in Beverly Hills, she wore a pastel-pink Donna Karan outfit with red Fendi clog sandals. Her hair and make-up were breathtakingly perfect.

Yet, for all her neat and studied insouciance, the thing that most intrigued me was the necklace she wore. It was designed to form a sparkling, bejeweled logo that would shortly thereafter become familiar to millions the world over. At that time, however, I'd never seen it before.

"Every time I'd show up somewhere, the music fans would go, 'J Lo!' so it's kind of an *homage* to them," she explained, pronouncing it the French way ("ohm-maage"), rather nonchalantly. Ah, such casual panache, I remember thinking.

Not long after, of course, the album of the same name was released and she became a household word. A line of fragrances was launched bearing that same logo. Louis Vuitton signed her to an advertising contract. People still think of her in terms of a certain Versace dress. Her mother, Guadalupe Lopez, 58, made the news in April 2004, for playing dollar-slots at an Atlantic City casino and winning US$2.4 million. It was surely a windfall for her but a paltry sum compared with her famous daughter's income, estimated at the end of 2003 to hover around US$29 million.

Well, what's not to like about that? Women from all walks of life testify to being fans of her music, if not her movies. She has been the butt of jokes, so to speak, for her famous *derrière*, but some say she single-handedly brought back to fashion the look of the full-figured woman – a welcome respite after years of rail-thin, "heroin chic" models dominating the magazine ads.

J. Lo is a logo, and "Jenny from the block" has become a walking, talking, lifestyle-elevating brand. She symbolizes the needs of many, and shows us all just how far things have come since the seemingly oxymoronic phrase "entertainment industry" was invented. The movie mogul Jack Warner (as in Warner Brothers) once pooh-poohed the demise of the silent movie era ("Who wants to see actors talk in films?" he actually said). Nobody could have predicted how this thing once half-derisively dubbed "show business" would someday become a multi-billion dollar machine into which the aspirations of so many are fed.

Entertainers deal in such intangible currency, selling our hopes and dreams (and even our memories, back to us), for which they are handsomely paid in cold, hard cash. And in today's overcrowded marketplace, how they deliver this is the business of branding.

Driven to distraction

In her book *Postcards From the Edge*, the actress Carrie Fisher drolly lampooned Hollywood and the vagaries of the entertainment industry. "Show business," she wrote, "it's only about distraction. Being transported out of your life, having someone else's life for a while, identifying with them, feeling relief that their predicament isn't yours or feeling relief that it is. A way of dreaming outside your head."

These days, we dream waking dreams, fueled by memories of the places we've been transported to by the people we've seen. We've assigned desirable values to these people. We've ascribed emotions to their images and used them as a scrim for our personal projections. How else can one explain the impact of Elvis Presley and the Beatles? They weren't just entertainers, they were social phenomena aided by the timely arrival of television into millions of American households. They were the fitting answer to the angst of the repressive Eisenhower era. And later, when Vietnam, Watergate, and the Sixties counterculture took hold, sweeping changes occurred and we feel their impact, even today.

Lives had changed, because people had become brands.

In an earlier and perhaps more innocent time, the very idea of movie stars influencing people's lives would have been laughed at. Now, in the early years of the twenty-first century, there are people like Father Richard Leonard, an Australian and a Jesuit priest, who has completed a doctorate in film studies at the University of Melbourne and has publicly stated his belief that the cinema has now replaced the church, as a place for people to "encounter otherness" and seek "ethical formation" and thus experience "a sense of God." He is an avowed fan of what he calls "mystical directors" – his favorites are Alfred Hitchcock, Bernardo Bertolucci, Martin Scorsese, and Peter Weir – and he has even made short films himself at the London Film School. He told the *Sydney Morning Herald*, "If we are waiting for people to come back to church, we could be waiting for a long time. Maybe we should go where they are and speak in a language that they now understand, which is the language of the cinema."

Contrast that with the example of the Spanish film director Pedro Almodóvar, whose film *Bad Education* opened the 2004 Cannes Film Festival. The film was about the controversial topic of sexual abuse by Catholic priests, and Almodóvar gave interviews in which he personally castigated the Catholic church for its hypocrisy. "I think the worst thing that has happened to the Catholic religion, which is a wonderful invention, is having priests teach," he told *Newsweek*. "I personally was not abused by any of these priests, but because in school we told each other everything, we all knew what was going on.... The more people hear about these cases – that 11,000 cases have been reported in the United States – the more people will denounce it. I don't know if my film will help. I hope it does."

How many Catholics will revise their views of their religion because of Pedro Almodóvar? Or, for that matter, how many smokers will quit the habit after supermodel Christy Turlington's no-smoking campaigns? Many who are cynical about celebrities involving themselves in social advocacy might well scoff at Sting's outcry at the decimation of Amazon rainforests or Angelina Jolie for pointing out the plight of children in Third World countries, but the United Nations has a habit of conferring "Goodwill ambassador" titles on people whom they know will be heard – like the Norwegian actress Liv Ullmann and the English singer (and former Spice Girl) Geri Halliwell, although nothing quite beats the fact that Angelina Jolie was personally given, by no less than UN Secretary-General Kofi Annan, a "Citizen of the World" award in October 2003. It's almost as if celebrities themselves confer a sheen of respectability on otherwise ignored causes. Because these people exist in the general public's mind as veritable brands, their endorsement helps give their causes the necessary push.

All this points to the fact that people are socially conditioned to see certain traits in others as desirable, and to expect that the celebrities they worship maintain such excellent attributes. Actresses like Marilyn Monroe and supermodels like Kate Moss are considered more attractive than most because they typify women whose waists are 70 percent the size of their hips – the socially acceptable epitome, according to the experts. The Brazilian supermodel Gisele Bundchen has an exceptional BMI ("body mass index" – the medical standard for measuring a person's body fat based on his or her height and weight). Where the average BMI is anywhere from 18.5 to 20, Gisele's is 16. Given her frame – tall and slim with large breasts – she would be considered perfectly proportioned. On a normal person, however, a BMI of 16 would mean small hips and a flat chest. This makes Gisele something of an anomaly, though it is the very thing that makes her so prized.

Indeed, so many elements of human nature are factors in the arena of celebrity worship, and their very ubiquity enables the machinery of celebrity to function. Glamour, it is said, is the quality of evoking envy – a nice thing to have if you're an actor, musician, or model, since it gets you good tables in restaurants, provided you can parlay that quality into a career. But the days of beautifully backlit sirens like Jayne Mansfield and Rita Hayworth are long gone, and the face of what elicits envy has evolved. The kind of buttons that today's icons push go beyond mere envy. Madonna and Britney Spears push buttons related to a range of vicarious pleasures, rooted in such unspeakable things like Judaeo-Christian guilt and the mass-market proliferation of softcore pornography – not a bad thing if you know how to milk it as a cash cow, even if parents of teenage girls might beg to differ.

How and why this has happened is the very focus of this book.

And how more timely could this phenomenon be? Everyone now knows what Andy Warhol said, that everyone in the future will be "famous for 15 minutes." But we didn't fully understand just how ahead of his time he was, since no one could have predicted the sheer explosion of mass media that has become the norm today.

"There's going to be a new movement and a new kind of person and you could be that person," Warhol said, and immediately we can think of the way "reality television" has dramatically revolutionized the way we see the world. If once unknown wannabes could be transported out of their bathrooms where they used to do their singing, zooming into the stratosphere to morph into recording stars like Kelly Clarkson, Ruben Stoddard, and Fantasia Barrino (the winners of the first three seasons of *American Idol*), then the sky's the limit. Shy men now root for the hapless geeks in *Average Joe*, where ordinary Joe Schmoes can vie for the attention of bodacious babes and feel like Brad Pitt for a day. Or, if you get lucky, the duration of a television season.

Image as brand, idol as icon

What this book does, then, is examine the extent of such hero worship, by analyzing the intriguing relationship between global celebrity culture and the phenomenon of branding. There is a sense of wonderment in the way certain people have become commodified into products, so as to achieve the kind of cross-cultural success that transcends geographical and geopolitical borders, even if what's being sold sometimes is only the sizzle and not the steak.

Some people have become known for their images, and they have then become co-opted into the mechanism of consumer culture by way of branding. The best of these are celebrities who have become household names, reaching audiences well beyond their own chosen crafts – the likes of Madonna, David Bowie, Bob Dylan, and Bob Marley, for instance, who are all known outside the music world. Others have made credible inroads outside their own countries, like the Japanese rock band Shonen Knife and pretty female singers like Hikaru Utada, Namie Amuro, and Ayumi Hamasaki, as well as Canadian singers Avril Lavigne and Celine Dion, and the Australian dance diva Kylie Minogue.

Then there are those ubiquitous celebrity endorsements, commonly seen in magazines. The sports world, of course, has long been populated with them: Tiger Woods and Michael Jordan have been associated with Nike, Andre Agassi with his Aramis Life fragrance, the

Formula One racing car driver Juan Pablo Montoya posed with an Audemars Piguet watch named after him (with Hewlett-Packard logos all over his racing outfit), and so on. Marketers call this kind of thing "brand extension" – the process by which a certain brand is retrofitted to suit other kinds of practical use (in the manner that Dunhill, for instance, makes not only cigarettes but also fragrances).

Jennifer Lopez, with her apparel and fragrance lines and her ads for Louis Vuitton, remains a highly viable commercial entity. This induces large questions pertaining to how her public profile is managed and maintained. How much money gets made? Who really benefits? How long will such linkage last? And why should anyone care, given the vast wasteland of marketing flops amid today's climate of competitive clamor?

In this age of technological breakthroughs, precipitated by the Internet, all bets are off. The Australian band Jet became a hit sensation in the United States without ever playing there, thanks to their song "Are You Gonna Be My Girl?" being featured in an *iPod* television commercial, which led to the song itself becoming one of the hottest paid-for digital downloads ever. The 15-gigabyte iPod that holds 3,000 songs is already *passé*, since 60-gigabyte models from a number of competing companies have already come onto the market. A whole 70-minute compact disc can be downloaded in a mere ten minutes.

And one thing is for certain: Those Britney Spears websites are not going to go away. Indeed, one of the most intriguing aspects of the celebrity machine has been the use of sexuality in image creation. An American sex toy company has even named one of its vibrators after Angelina Jolie; the item can be bought through its online shop, a unique "brand extension" exercise, the kind aligned with modern marketing buzzwords like "mindshare" and "namespace."

It has become a very crowded world in the pop culture universe, and everyone is fighting for a piece of the pie. Why else would someone as legendary as Madonna continue to pursue commercial interests beyond music and film? Cynics would say it's altogether too convenient for her to become the poster girl for motherhood, since she has been publishing children's books and has even launched a line of children's clothing (including miniskirts and see-through tops for young girls). But her fans will surely choose to see it another way: that her marketing savvy is admirable, since she has been extending her status as a role model by putting her lifestyle on the line, demonstrating that all women can empower themselves by being a mother like her. Madonna remains one of the most potent examples of how modern celebrities have shaped modern lifestyles through their branding.

In essence, the fact that whole lives can be changed this way refutes the claims made by the likes of Naomi Klein (author of the anti-branding book, *No Logo*), since most celebrities exist to fulfill a demand created by market forces. Most brands exist because people really do want them. Lots of social scientists have studied the dynamics of modern-day consumerism (most notably James Twitchell, author of *Lead Us Into Temptation: The triumph of American materialism*), but almost everyone has repeated the truisms of Andy Warhol, who "called upon everything that he had learned from advertising and television, where the dollar sign and the gun were the predominant symbols, and the common denominator was to arouse sexual desires without satisfying them and to shock," as Victor Bockris noted in his famous biography, *Warhol*.

This notion has permeated modern life today in so many ways. It can best be viewed through the prism of trends inspired by celebrities in fashion (like the anorexic-thin "heroin chic" look inspired by supermodel Kate Moss in those Calvin Klein ads, which have since given way to the resurrection of the full-figured woman thanks to Jennifer Lopez). The Malaysian, New York-based supermodel Ling has been photographed for Gucci and Clinique, and since she gets paid a mere US$15,000 a day, has surely done her share to alter the perception of Asian women in the West, as have the Canadian-born, Hong Kong actress Christy Chung with her line of slimming salon advertisements for *Marie France Bodyline* across Asia, and others like them.

The plethora of products that have invaded the global marketplace has in part caused the surge in celebrity worship, as companies scramble for suitable figures to translate their advertising and publicity into fortunes at the cash register. Hype is used to sell hope. We are urged to buy casual clothes (David Bowie and his wife Iman in multiple-page magazine inserts for Tommy Hilfiger; full-page ads for Gap clothing with rising stars like Joss Stone and Taryn Manning). The very rifeness of the competition is illustrated by some startling examples. Jessica Riddle, for instance, remains a young and gifted but still unknown singer songwriter, but she was accorded the privilege of a contract with the fashion house Givenchy, in tandem with the release of her debut album *Key of a Minor* in 2000 on the Hollywood Records label.

Clearly some marketing person had thought Riddle's good looks would dovetail nicely with the kind of aspirational appeal that Givenchy had with young women. Curiously, Hollywood Records would shortly later succeed in making a pop star out of Hilary Duff, due no doubt to her teen-queen movie stardom. (And why Jessica did not similarly succeed is, well, still something of a riddle.)

Even a more adult-oriented chanteuse like Sarah McLachlan found herself branded in such terms; her latest album *Afterglow* is sold in Asia in an elegantly boxed version containing her CD along with discount vouchers from The Natural Source (a retailer of Australian "naturopathic" beauty products) and the wellness company Spa Esprit, reflecting marketers' intentions to tie her soothing soft-rock sounds to the needs of women who enjoy beauty and spa treatments.

The potential impact of such events cannot be underestimated. In 1999, the music of the late British singer/songwriter Nick Drake underwent an unexpected revival in America when his song "Pink Moon" was used in a Volkswagen commercial, and sales of both his records and the cars soared – a whole 25 years after his death. The most bizarre endeavor, however, was the appearance of Bob Dylan in a series of commercials for Victoria's Secret. Most Dylan fans, used to his ironic wit, expressed bemusement when it was announced in April 2004 that his song "Love Sick," from his 1997 Grammy-winning album *Time Out of Mind*, would play in the background (in 15-, 30- and 60-second versions!), as model Adriana Lima strolled through Venice clad in just bra, panties, and spike heels. Dylan was approached directly by the lingerie company and readily agreed to appear, to the amazement of even the company's creative director.

Style counsel

Consider also the fact that in March 2004, *Yahoo!* in Great Britain polled 1,000 Internet users, asking which British person they would choose to represent Earth, should aliens ever land on this planet. The vote was won by Ozzy Osbourne, the eccentric rock star, made doubly famous in recent years by his "family reality" television show, *The Osbournes*. Certainly one could hardly find a more "aspirational" figure, given that Osbourne was an abattoir worker and convicted burglar prior to gaining fame as the lead singer of the rock band Black Sabbath. (The same poll results showed Prime Minister Tony Blair emerging third and *American Idol* judge Simon Cowell resoundingly last.)

This was a publicity godsend for Osbourne, since a new eight-CD anthology called *Black Box* was about to be released, and two former roadies of the band had just published their racy tour memoirs (a book entitled *How Black Was My Sabbath*), further securing Osbourne's place in pop culture history (and ensuring the wrath of more parents with pot-smoking, head-banging kids).

Nothing seems too absurd to champion, clearly, in this age of instant gratification. But how did we get here? We can ponder (or shudder) over the endorsements that failed *American Idol* performer William Hung will continue to get (now that he has actually released a surprise hit album and endorsed a slimming tea product). Michael Jackson and Britney Spears were chosen to represent "the Pepsi Generation." ("When it comes to image making, PepsiCo is one of the smartest companies around," noted *Fortune* magazine, which devoted a fascinating article in its April 4, 2004 issue to the company's "brand makeover.") Jackson's star, however, has fallen considerably since news of his child molestation charges. ("Several potentially lucrative business deals that were in the offing have since evaporated," as the *New York Times* reported on April 24, 2004.)

Our lifestyles, whether they hinge on the consumption of soft drinks or designer clothes, have been inexorably altered by the way celebrities are used to sell us visions of ourselves. "Creativity is the heart of personal style; self-acceptance is its soul," wrote image consultant and style guru Carla Mathis in her classic stylist's textbook, *The Triumph of Individual Style*, but what celebrities do is mirror our own sense of self-acceptance and self-esteem.

Some people have taken this to ridiculous limits. Twin brothers Matt and Mike Schlepp paid for US$37,000 of plastic surgery so they could look like Brad Pitt, and Jennifer Sandifer had a bodylift so she could resemble Kate Winslet. All this was shown on the new MTV reality show *I Want a Famous Face*, which debuted in March 2004 and took top place in the US cable ratings – proof positive that celebrity images have never been as profoundly visible or perversely effective, even if we feel that the chimera of idol worship must have reached a zenith.

Given such global potential, how could anyone blame Marina Golbahari, the 13-year-old star of the acclaimed Afghan film *Osama* (Golden Globe winner for best foreign film), for telling the *New York Times*, "I'd like to be a big star in America"? We now live in a new world order, where Hollywood movie stars are seen in Japanese commercials (hawking products they don't even use), and major American entertainment companies have strategically invested in new theme parks in China (Universal in Shanghai, Disney in Hong Kong, where Disneyland is scheduled to open in early 2006), paving the way for the imminent explosion of the world's largest consumer market. Elsewhere in Asia, those who can't seem to pronounce "Catherine Zeta-Jones" continue to buy Elizabeth Arden skin renewal serum, inspired by her sultry visage and the slogan, "New overnight success."

But success is never sudden. Much thought has been devoted to placing products within the willing scrutiny of any target market. All the wicked wit and pleasurable sensations of pop culture are brought to bear, in ways as never before, in a deception partaken by the willing. Unraveling the mysteries and deciphering the metaphysics of such desire, however ambitious, is the real goal of this book.

Malcolm Gladwell wrote of similar things in *The Tipping Point*, an influential tome that shows how some ideas become widely disseminated like epidemics, getting "sticky" because they speak to people's deep-seated, innermost needs. Framing this phenomenon entirely within the realm of the entertainment arena raises the bar a little higher – because of the insidious confluence of money and marketing.

"You're talking about the curiosity that comes with me," Traci Lords told me, back in 1994, when we discussed the role of fame in her life. "I would never stand in line and get an autograph. I would never save an autograph. I don't understand any of that, I really don't. I sign autographs, and it makes me feel ridiculous. I think it's very flattering, but I just find it completely shocking. It's like, why do they want this? I don't understand it, really. I don't get that part of it at all." But her fans do. This was, of course, before she transcended adult-film notoriety to become the star of the sci-fi action series *First Wave* (a journey chronicled in her remarkable 2003 autobiography *Underneath It All*).

The real star of this book is that very "curiosity," how it is manufactured and then nurtured, however naughty or nice the star in question. It's the same kind of thing that led the very wholesome Sandra Bullock to be called "the new Doris Day," just as the publicity machine for her aptly titled film *Miss Congeniality* was nicely revving up. *Que sera sera*: whatever will be, will be.

Artifice and illusion can be comforting indeed, but how and why have they become so valuable, so sought-after, in our hierarchy of human needs? Many inquiring minds, I believe, want to know.

Linda Bladholm

Linda Bladholm is a food critic and columnist with the *Miami Herald*. Prior to that, she was a magazine photographer and had worked with many celebrities, both in her native Chicago and also in Manchester, England, where she previously lived. She is the author of the cult classic *The Asian Grocery Store Demystified*, published by Renaissance Books in 1999, inspired by a decade of living in Japan and Singapore.

You've dined at Larios, which is Gloria and Emilio Estefan's restaurant in Miami. What's your impression?

The Estefans must be doing something right. Every time I have gone there, the place is packed with Cuban-Americans enjoying the atmosphere as well as the typically well-executed Cuban-style dishes. I think they are justified in being in the restaurant business. They have hired quality cooks and that shows they know what they're doing. The downfall of most celebrity restaurants is that they don't understand that the food has to be good. The name will bring people once, but if they don't have a pleasant experience or enjoy the food, they won't come back.

You photographed rock stars before you became a food writer. Any favorite memories to share?

I remember Alice Cooper, who was not scary at all. He talked mostly about golf and he had his pet snake with him, which was quite tame. Liz Phair was wonderful. The day I went to shoot her was below freezing in Chicago, and she agreed to pose outside and was very natural, relaxed, and down-to-earth, incredibly easy to work with. She was a real pro and that made it a fun shoot despite the cold. I got the sense that she was a woman on the brink, dealing with sudden success very well while keeping her image under her control as much as she could.

What do you think of the way "celebrity branding" is going?

There isn't the calibre of stars like there used to be. I don't think you can compare thug gangsta-rappers with diamonds in their teeth to people like Sophia Loren or even Madonna. You don't even have to have talent these days to be a celebrity! Like Paris Hilton – what is she famous for? Being an heiress and being in sex videos with former boyfriends! I may be bored with the whole celebrity scene but most people can't get enough, especially here in South Beach, Miami. People with no lives of their own fill the emptiness with following celebrities. It's like celebrities have replaced religion.

What do you think of fame as applied to celebrity chefs like Anthony Bourdain, Keith Floyd, Jamie Oliver, Nigella Lawson, Elizabeth David, and the late Julia Child?

I find it fascinating that chefs have celebrity status and are stars in their own right. But it depends on the chef. Some no longer cook and open a zillion branches, like Nobu, though I still like his food. Anthony Bourdain is entertaining, and what's not to like about Jamie Oliver and Nigella Lawson? I loved Julia Child and am a big fan of Elizabeth David – she really opened the door to good food and cooking being a respectable thing to be passionate about. What I liked most about both Elizabeth David and Julia Child was that they were not pretentious. I'd like to think I am that way too.

Who has been your favorite food celebrity to work with?

Ruth Reichl, the editor-in-chief of *Gourmet* magazine. She was very warm, very easy to pose and photograph. She told me privacy is overrated – a refreshing view on life as a celebrity.

Do you feel like you have been made into a celebrity yourself?

Yes, being a *Miami Herald* columnist and author has pushed me into minor celebrity status, at least here in Miami, although my books have cult fans all over the place. I even get e-mails from England. I try not to abuse my status by taking freebies or attending parties I won't be writing about. I know who my real friends are and who is trying to use me, for PR purposes or whatever. It's still strange being recognized in the post office!

2
John Candy Sat Here: Celebrity and the Movies

Jerry Stahl, the writer who famously parlayed his own memoirs of drug addiction into a Hollywood movie called *Permanent Midnight*, once talked in an interview about coming to terms with celebrityhood.

"My first encounter with fame when I came to Hollywood," he recalled, "was when my ex-wife was working at a producer's house that used to be John Candy's home. When I sat on the toilet seat, I thought, 'John Candy sat here.'"

Sometimes, when one actually lives in Hollywood, it's easy to forget that celebrities are people too. I once did a double-take when I stopped my car at a red light and saw that the person driving the car next to mine was Jamie Lee Curtis. I did the same when I was walking down El Camino Drive in Beverly Hills and saw Glenn Close pulling out of the parking garage of the William Morris Agency. (So very cool, I thought, these people drive their own cars!) I even nearly met Jack Nicholson once at a party. Jack looked at me from across the crowded room and smiled his famous Cheshire cat smile, the kind that ate the camera in *The Shining*. I smiled back and nodded, and he nodded too. But something in his nod said not to come any closer. And so I didn't. To this day I still don't know why, but I marvel at Jack's non-verbal facility. He just wanted to sip his martini and not be bothered by total strangers. And understandably so. Who was I to make his fabulous acquaintance?

"How do we begin to covet?" the serial killer Hannibal Lecter famously quoted Marcus Aurelius, in *The Silence of the Lambs*. "We begin by coveting what we see every day."

Nowhere is that statement made more incisively poignant than in the very medium that brought it to the masses. Film as an art form has invaded our lives and defined our collective thoughts so powerfully that, arguably, most people still fail to grasp completely the sheer impact of what they see. The legendary figures that certain actors portray are merely one part of what makes this illusion possible, since they provide the template for osmosis, invading the subconscious mind and reaching areas that civilized society might prefer us not to reach.

Some people, however, refuse to go gentle into that good night.

One of these people is Sir David Puttnam, the British film producer, who wrote *Movies and Money*, one of the finest books about the business. Originally published in the UK in 1997 as *The Undeclared War: The struggle for control of the world's film industry*, it celebrated the magic of moving images by documenting the medium's long and colorful history, while also positing a profoundly disturbing argument. Puttnam, well known for confronting the kinds of tough topics depicted in his films (Oscar winners like *Chariots of Fire* and *The Killing Fields*, and cult classics like *Local Hero* and *Midnight Express*) had a personal agenda: he sought to solve a major problem facing Europe, a whole continent of filmmakers fighting a losing battle against the dominance of American films.

"Hollywood movies accounted for 80 percent of box-office revenues across much of Europe," he observed, while "films produced in Europe accounted for less than one percent of the American box office." This startling imbalance wasn't helped by the fact that even in 1997, some 40 percent of revenues of the American film and television industry were earned overseas, with more than half that total coming from Europe. "Entertainment had become America's second largest export, after aircraft manufacturing," Puttnam added. "The American film and television industry brought back US$3.5 billion a year in surplus balance of payments to the United States."

A long-time fan of Hollywood films himself, despite his brief and troubled tenure as head of Columbia Pictures (from 1986 to 1988), Puttnam concluded that European filmmakers only had themselves to blame. Why on earth did millions of people flock to theatres to see *Jurassic Park*? European auteurs were all becoming dinosaurs themselves, Puttnam believed. In slaving away to produce brilliant if brooding works mirroring the human condition, the Jean-Luc Godards and Ingmar Bergmans of the world had somehow ignored something equally important.

That was the strange and wondrous thing called marketing. They had been so true to the craft, they had forgotten the audience.

Magnification of the self

The Americans knew better, and that legacy has remained with us today. Humphrey Bogart stares pensively in black and white splendor in a print ad for Longines watches, bearing the slogan: "Elegance is an attitude." (Longines has been the hallmark of elegance since 1832, it also reminds us.) Marilyn Monroe's visage stares out from an ad for US Bank in Santa Monica, California, in a 2001 campaign announcing the institution's renaming. (The caption read "Norma Jean Baker" in bold type, followed by "At Santa Monica Bank, our name changed too.") Steve McQueen is still used to promote TAG Heuer watches, reprising his classic auto-racing film *Le Mans* (some 30 years later) and his own penchant for Formula One driving.

What these do, pointedly, is assure us that consumers can assume the quiet confidence of Bogart and Monroe and McQueen by buying into those products. Allure by association is alive and well, even if all three stars are dead.

"Such magnification of the self is unique to cinema," Sir David Puttnam noted. "As a boy, I would sit in the darkness and soak up the images and ideas of films like Fred Zinnemann's *The Search*, Elia Kazan's *On the Waterfront* and Stanley Kramer's *Inherit the Wind*. Those films were my education. I wanted to express the humanism of Montgomery Clift caring for that boy in *The Search*; I allowed James Dean to work out my adolescent complexities and frustration in *East of Eden*. It was from films like these that almost every tenet by which I have tried to live somehow evolved.

"As a result of the intoxicating impact of those movies, the first day that I went to America, in 1963, was, in many ways, the most exciting of my life. Part of me was coming home. That's how powerful the impact of American cinema had been on me. Far more than any other influence, more even than school, my family, my attitudes, dreams, preconceptions and pre-conditions for life had been irreversibly shaped five and a half thousand miles away in a balmy suburb of Los Angeles called Hollywood."

What that balmy suburb has best perfected is the selling of our dreams. Every time we pay for a movie ticket, our dreams are being sold back to us. We later revisit them on DVD, staring bug-eyed in rapt attention as all those menus and sub-menus play out behind-the-scenes action, with cast and crew interviews and, on occasion, preciously salvaged outtakes and bloopers that remind us of the sublime nature of artifice. And we can't ever get enough.

How could it be otherwise? From this montage of memories dwelling in our deepest recesses arise all the cool images we retain, personified in Brad Pitt and Julia Roberts and Tom Cruise and Sharon Stone, telling us we need to choose to be more like them, if we're smart enough to know how.

There are superficial ways of learning this, of course, and we see it all the time, in photos of film stars gliding down the red carpet at Cannes – Uma Thurman in Jean-Paul Gaultier, Charlize Theron in Vera Wang, Adrien Brody in his Ermenegildo Zegna ads ("which makes me feel validated, even though I buy Zegna all the time," an advertising executive from Chicago once told me). What we covet isn't so much the expensive apparel but the intangible sense of attitude that these stars ooze.

On a deeper level, we all attempt to uncover for ourselves just what makes these people seem so eminently desirable, as if we can never be as good-looking or as good as they appear. "Truth is a judgement about surfaces," some sage once remarked, though it's really the very surface calm emanating from these actors that we admire.

Seduction of the spirit

"He's a very unusual man, he's bigger than life, both offscreen and on," the producer Arnold Kopelson once told me, when I asked him about working with the other, more famous Arnold, the one who would some years later become the Governor of California. Kopelson had just come off the success of producing the Harrison Ford thriller *The Fugitive*, and he had placed Schwarzenegger in the suspense thriller *Eraser*.

"I was fortunate," Kopelson recalled. "We get 50 to 100 screenplays a week in my office. When *Eraser* came along, I couldn't think of a better actor in the world market to play someone like this. I worked on the screenplay for three months on my own, got it into better shape, and then I brought it to Arnold. It started off a four-month process where I worked with him nearly every day. We worked on it together and we shaped that character to be Arnold Schwarzenegger. And that's really how it goes."

"We had an explosion where we were 60 feet away from the blast and Arnold jumps out of a 747. That posed a problem because this is a live-action film and Arnold likes to do his own stunts. So I walked onto the set one day and they're about to hoist him 50 feet up in the air. I said, 'What are you doing?' He said, 'I'm going to do this.' I said, 'No, you're not.' He said, 'Sure, I am. I'm going to do it. Don't worry about it.' And I said, 'Arnold, I don't care about you getting killed. I care about my movie.'"

"He laughed, and said, 'Don't worry, I've done this before.' They hoisted him up on this very thin cable – you can barely see it – and he had a little, flimsy harness and he literally jumped into a free fall, out of a fuselage of a 747 that was set up behind a soundstage in Hollywood. I always think worst-case, like what happens if the cable snaps. Making a movie like this, there can always be lots of problems. But Arnold's a big sport, and he really does like to do most of his own stunts."

The very believability of what audiences see is what endears certain actors to them. This is conveyed by word of mouth by moviegoers, and also by reviewers who have seen the film. Movie studio publicists love churning out press releases to the newspapers, magazines, and broadcasting stations about the real-life, death-defying stunts being done by stars, and this translates into a leap of faith, whereby fans are made and an action star's branding is created.

The likes of Arnold Schwarzenegger, Sylvester Stallone, and Jackie Chan have all benefited from such publicity. The resulting star charisma is an obvious intangible that money cannot truly buy, even though the stars themselves are always handsomely paid for it. The Austrian government even created an official postage stamp in honor of their country's biggest Hollywood star, released on July 30, 2004,

Schwarzenegger's 57th birthday. The stamp, valued at US$1.25, shows him in a suit and tie, with the American and Austrian flags in the background, part of a stamp series called "Austrians living abroad." It was not the first local honor bestowed on the muscleman from Graz; a sports stadium in his hometown had already been named after him.

This, naturally, points to a branding phenomenon unique to celebrities – their drawing power lies in the way people have identified with particular characters they've played. Some movie stars do survive and sometimes even transcend a scandalous persona, which in part helps to escalate their fame. The best example might well be Sharon Stone after her famous panty-less, leg-crossing scene in *Basic Instinct*. (When asked about it in one interview, Stone said, "You know, my feeling, beginning with *Basic Instinct*, is best summed up by a phone call my mother got from her girlfriend, who said, 'How do you feel about your daughter playing a lesbian?' and my mother said, 'You know, somehow I'm much more concerned about her playing a sociopathic serial killer.'")

Fame is the business of perpetuating myth, and one's myth needs to be kept consistent with public perception. In other words, it takes a star of such regally devil-may-care bearing as Sharon Stone to shrug off the naysayers. If you project the attitude that people can believe whatever they want, the end result is usually that people believe what they're supposed to. Stone's character, Catherine Trammell, in *Basic Instinct* is the very kind of sexually voracious woman who will drive men crazy if she's not wearing underwear, and so we admire her intrepid sensibility and condone her free spirit. The proof was certainly in the pudding, because that movie secured Stone's career and made her a star.

Another example is John Woo, the Hong Kong director who moved to Hollywood to work with the likes of John Travolta and Nicolas Cage after years of perfecting the hard-boiled *film noir* genre, via stories of conflicted cops and Hong Kong Triad gangsters. I met and interviewed Woo in 1986, and we were discussing his body of work with the actor Chow Yun-fat, the debonair "Alain Delon of Asia," when I asked him about making movies around grim tales of

Hong Kong "Triad" (gangster) warfare and his preference for certain recurring themes: friendship, loyalty, trust, betrayal.

Such themes, he told me, were "the most important thing" about his movies. They were what made his movies unique and special, more than the incessant gunfire often featured in his films. They were the hallmarks of his branding.

"Much of it comes from what I call the spirit of the Chinese knight," he explained. "The spirit of chivalry. When I was a child, after we moved from China to Hong Kong, we were very poor. I grew up in a slum. My parents couldn't afford to send me to school till I was nine years old. We were very fortunate, we were so lucky, to get support from an American family. They sent money through a church to support my school fees. That's how I got my education. So I always have a kind of appreciation to anyone who gave us help. After I entered the film business, I got a lot of help from friends. When I was down, I got a lot of support from [fellow director] Tsui Hark. And then we worked together to make *A Better Tomorrow*. That movie took me to the top. That movie changed my life. But before *A Better Tomorrow*, when Tsui Hark was down and I was quite popular, I helped him get started again.

"This kind of real friendship, helping each other, appreciating each other, I always like to put in my movies. In my movies, the knight characters – their behaviour, their thoughts, their feelings – they all come from real life. Not the Triad thing. Actually, I know nothing about Triad wars. That's just my imagination. I use that as background. But the feelings, the emotions, they come from real life."

It may seem prosaic and mundane, but Chow Yun-Fat has also publicly expressed concern about the use of Triad gangsters in Woo's films. In Canadian film critic Christopher Heard's book *Ten Thousand Bullets: The cinematic journey of John Woo*, published in 2000, Chow related that he was quite disturbed that he was being seen by some as a role model for Hong Kong Triad members. Studies in Hong Kong had shown that, however coincidentally, Triad membership had gone up with the popularity of John Woo's films. "Yes, that really did bother me," Chow said, while shooting the 1992 Woo film *Hard Boiled*. "I was very concerned. So I told John Woo that with this film, he would have to turn that around. I wanted *Hard Boiled* to be about a bond between policemen, and to try to make that a life just as heroic and appealing to the young people."

The need to make his characters heroic and appealing, despite appalling circumstances (brothers and friends get maimed or killed, a frequent recurrence in the pre-Hollywood John Woo canon) is the very same call as that enshrined in the spirit of the Chinese knight. An enterprising advertising agency took advantage of this some years later, when Woo's own life was mined commercially: In an ad for Mercedes-Benz, a luxury sedan with the famous three-pointed star is seen driving through a Hong Kong slum, with the accompanying copy noting that this was the neighborhood Woo grew up in.

Make hit movies and you too can be driving a Mercedes, it appears to be saying, not at all disclosing the ultimate irony – John Woo himself does not drive. (He has never learned to; his wife Annie still drives him around when they are in Los Angeles, and he has openly admitted to reporters that he is terrified of being on the freeways, even as a passenger.)

Welcome to the machine

There is a fascinating flow chart that delineates the way films are made into hits, and actors into film stars. In the United States, the publicity machine works in a two-fold manner: through the media and at the box office. The area of intersect is large even though anomalies do occur; some actors become stars even though their movies are flops, and some filmmakers will directly influence the outcome in aggressively overt ways. In 2004, for instance, the actor-director Vincent Gallo personally paid for billboards advertising his film *The Brown Bunny*, which also gained endless reams of press thanks to a controversial sex scene (in which Gallo was fellated onscreen by his then-girlfriend, Chloë Sevigny), although such sensational episodes are usually rare.

Box-office numbers theoretically reflect the monetary success of a film in terms of ticket sales. When moviegoers purchase tickets, individual theatres collect three kinds of information: how much money is in the cash register, how many tickets were sold, and of those sold, how many were full-price admissions and how many discounted admissions. The "box-office receipts" that are tallied and sent to the studio as reports only deal with the first – money actually collected at the ticket booth. Information on the number and types of tickets sold is transmitted more slowly, by a different process altogether. Theatres submit reports on these only when their contracts obligate them to pay the studios. The necessary paperwork can take up to two months.

What this archaic system creates is a situation whereby the movie studios, lacking real-time admissions information, have to quickly decide how to allocate resources – millions of dollars in advertising, to begin with – within hours of a movie opening, often based on incomplete information. One side-effect of this phenomenon, by which large numbers of tickets are sold every opening weekend all across the United States, is the frenzied approach that the publicity machine takes in order to court the media.

In Hollywood, people who work "media relations" (as opposed to the more generic "public relations") are called "publicists." They are hired to generate "buzz" through issuing press releases and setting up press interviews. The long, insane hours they work sometimes include the kind of overtime never experienced in the lives of ordinary working stiffs, since they're often expected to set up and then attend publicity-related events like "press screenings" (special screenings of a movie for reporters and reviewers) and "press junkets" (travel-related schemes to woo the newspapers and magazines, like the one Disney staged for its US$140m war epic *Pearl Harbor*, in which the members of the media were feted on board a real Second World War battleship in Hawaii).

Publicists have a distinct advantage over mere mortals – they get to deal directly with their celebrity clients, although sometimes a circuitous route is necessary depending on how many assistants (and other "handlers") a star employs. Requests for press interviews, for example, are given to publicists who then have to channel them through whatever system of protocol has been set up – usually the star's manager or management team is the final arbiter of whether the interview happens or not, unless of course there are controversial issues involved, in which case the star in question might overrule his or her managers (as in cases when certain stars refuse to give interviews to certain publications for political or personal reasons). Certain topics can also be decreed off-limits, and this usually happens when certain stars find themselves embroiled in sex scandals or other gossip-friendly news (Jennifer Lopez doesn't much care to discuss her former husbands, Winona Ryder probably feels the same about discussing shoplifting, and certain others are loath to answer questions about their sexual orientation).

The basic idea is to present as far as possible a series of portraits favorable to the studio, in order to best promote a given film. This is how people are turned into "personalities," with the charm-school switch flicked on. A star can then become a reporter's new best friend for the 20 minutes or hour designated as interview time. Tom Cruise will turn on his charm and flash that megawatt lady-killer smile for the cameras, the kind that "opens films" (industry jargon for the manner in which the sheer strength of a star's name-billing lures people to the theaters).

"Meg Ryan is the owner of one of the most expressive mouths in cinema," wrote Andrew Anthony of the venerable British newspaper the *Guardian*. "Wide and admirably flexible, it's a mouth that seldom gives up its lines without a struggle. A gape here, a grimace there, and just when it's shaped itself into a gash of speechless disappointment, out pops a piece of exquisitely timed dialogue. In short, it's a great comic mouth." Ryan probably never anticipated that her mouth would be the subject of that much scrutiny, but her onscreen persona is what makes her a shoo-in for all the "chick flick" roles.

That's her branding at work: America's sweetheart, in a wholesome yet modern way. The studios know women relate to her. When she is cast against type, bad reviews follow, as happened when she starred in Jane Campion's erotic thriller *In the Cut*, a role that should no doubt have gone to someone with a *femme fatale* flair like Lara Flynn Boyle. ("I'm the kind of woman who, when she walks into a party, all the other women leave the room," Boyle once quipped.

46

"Which makes me feel neither powerful nor insecure. It just makes me feel sad for the other women.") The screen siren *par excellence* Mae West, who knew about this sort of thing, once said, "It's better to be looked over than to be overlooked."

Yet where does the line divide, between illusion and reality? Even on something as mindless yet massively popular as the *Baywatch* television series, young women in awe of those bodacious lifeguards might think twice about squeezing into swimsuits if they knew what went into enhancing the female figure.

The show's big secret is actually a breast enhancer called Curves, made of medical-grade silicone gel and polyurethane, which molds to the shape of a woman's breasts in order to maximize the "jiggle factor" of the real thing. The *Baywatch* costume department uses it, but anyone can buy it, if they can afford it; Curves is sold in small, large, and extra large sizes, at US$129 a pair.

Regardless of how sublime might be the ridiculous, we look to film and television to tell us how to live, and we look to actors and actresses to tell us how to look. We buy the illusion and then buy magazines to tell us about the reality.

Bridget Fonda openly talked about the fake boobs she had to wear for the Quentin Tarantino film *Jackie Brown* ("I didn't have any modesty about the boobs, because they weren't mine"), had no problems portraying a socialite hooker in *Scandal* (playing Mandy Rice-Davies to Ian McKellen's John Profumo, in the 1989 film about the famous British sex-and-spy affair), and disclosed she is a vegetarian and loves Warner Bros. cartoons. That's how her image comes across in long feature pieces, like the one *Details* magazine did with her, in its February 1998 issue, neatly entitled "Confessions of a Dirty Blonde."

Another case study, more trenchantly so: Lucy Lawless, star of the hit series *Xena: Warrior Princess*, hosted a five-part documentary series on the Discovery Channel, aptly called *Warrior Women*. It was about the great female figures of the past 2,000 years, from Boudicca to Joan of Arc, and she admitted her pleasure with that piece of typecasting ("Who else were they going to call?" she laughed). In an interview with *Playboy* magazine, Lawless revealed several things that demonstrated just why the show's success was no fluke. Her warrior costume, for instance, was originally "black and malevolent. It had big claw-like epaulets and a cape. The producers thought it was too evil for a hero, so we changed it to brown and made it a little more audience-friendly."

"The current costume has a longer bodice, and it feels like my whole abdomen is in a straitjacket," she added. "The Wonderbra and the breastplate work together just fine. You can't have one without the other." And, for those wondering about her onscreen complexion, "I pushed for her to look busty and sexy and dark, like those statues in Madrid – big and curvaceous and bronzed.... So they paint on the tan with a sponge and it takes about five minutes." Times have certainly changed since James Bond introduced the world to women covered in gold paint, in *Goldfinger*.

Parasocial behavior

Celebrity branding is remarkably different from the way branding is applied to household goods. Household names are visible and present all the time, whereas celebrities sneak their way into our collective consciousness. We simmer with the heat of passion for our idols. It would all appear adolescent and mere piffle but for the fact that celebrityhood is a heavily monetized phenomenon. It was eye-opening enough in 1983 when 100 million viewers tuned in to watch the finale of the *M*A*S*H* television series (a cultural benchmark still only rivaled in America by the Super Bowl) but in 2004 the comedy series *Friends* had advertisers coughing up US$2 million per ad for the sitcom's last show, resulting in the studio, Warner Bros., pocketing an estimated US$2 billion in syndication sales (the second-highest after *Seinfeld*).

And what greater proof of success can you have than when your star Jennifer Aniston gets chosen to run carrying the Olympic torch to Athens for the 2004 summer games, thanks to her Greek (her real surname is Anastassakis) heritage ? Even her real-life husband, some guy named Brad Pitt, who played the Greek warrior Achilles in *Troy*, didn't qualify. (Aniston rivals Helen of Troy, surely, as the hairstyle that launched a thousand shampoos.)

So we covet what we see every day, and the star-making machine knows this. Branding is about seduction, lest we forget, and the key commodity is desire. Movie stars trade in this, and their stylishness is co-opted into mainstream imagery. "Teresa Heinz Kerry has presented herself to Americans as a multilingual free spirit, a woman with a taste for a 70s-era Jacqueline Bisset coiffure," noted fashion writer Ginia Bellafante in the *New York Times*, a mere three months before the 2004 US presidential election. Everything plays into the cultural sensibility that prizes certain kinds of looks, be it countenance or coiffure, as something attractive – to be shaped into something we all yearn for.

The fact that this is, of course, an artificial construct manufactured by those who control the selling of images isn't the point, as much as the fact of a marketplace that exists which fosters the need to encourage addiction. We want these stars. We want their branding. Because without them, we have seemingly lost a part of ourselves. Or so we are told, and so we accordingly believe.

"We call Hollywood 'Tinseltown' as if somehow it didn't matter," Sir David Puttnam reminded us. "Some try to persuade us that films and television are a business like any other. They are not. Films and television shape attitudes, create conventions of style and behavior, reinforce or undermine the wider values of society.... Creative artists, and those who work with them, have a heavy moral responsibility to challenge, inspire, question and affirm, as well as to entertain. Movies are more than fun, and more than big business. They are power."

And what the branding mechanism does brilliantly is harness that power, to the point where we now accept that we cannot live without it. To the point where we forget just who holds the power.

Think about this, the critics we read would exhort us, in terms of things like superheroes. How can anyone begin to explain, for instance, the fact that the first *Spider-Man* film took in a record US$114 million in its opening weekend in the United States alone, racking up a whopping US$406 million in the first week? The closest contenders in the box-office stakes were *Star Wars: Episode II – Attack of the Clones*, at US$310 million, and *Harry Potter and the Chamber of Secrets*, at US$210 million. Those are the kinds of figures that jolt the cynics, all those people who would dismiss comic book heroes or anything vaguely sci-fi (let alone sagas about teenage wizards) as juvenile junk.

Spider-Man and its 2004 sequel, *Spider-Man 2*, have been "really terrific," noted Jordan Raphael, co-author of *Stan Lee and the Rise and Fall of the American Comic Book* (2003). "There have only been three major superheroes in the 20th century – Superman, Batman and Spider-Man." The book sprang from a *Los Angeles Times Magazine* story Raphael wrote on the long life and career of Stanley Lieber, who had split his name to produce his famous pseudonym, and became famous as the creator of Spider-Man.

"I think comic-book writers have a legitimate place in the culture of celebrity," Raphael said. "When I became a journalist, I took every opportunity to write about comics in mainstream venues because I felt it was sort of a mission, to spread the gospel about this wonderful yet under-appreciated art form. Personally, I think comics have helped keep me young. On the other hand, they might have reduced my attention span and patience for longer works."

However, he admitted some bewilderment over the fans who swoon over meeting, say, Christopher Reeve because they wanted to meet Superman. "I don't go in for that kind of parasocial behavior," Raphael says. "I think if I actually met Superman – you know, the real Kryptonian in a blue-and-red costume – I would be thrilled. But the dudes who have portrayed him on film and on TV are not as cool."

Raphael has brought up a salient point: What are we really buying into when we buy the hype of celebrity? One true tale hints at the answer. In 1995, an executive with Boeing (who spoke for this book on condition of anonymity) was assigned the task of taking two VIPs on a personal tour of the company's premises. "I got stuck with squiring 'Randy Prince Andy' – Prince Andrew – and Charlton Heston around what was then the McDonnell Douglas facility in Long Beach, California, before Boeing took us over. The employees, thousands of them, had been prepped to shout their greetings and they did as we walked down the C-17 production line. However, the workers ignored Prince Andrew and crowded around Heston, who had been hired as part of a 'do' for a British trade event in Los Angeles. Heston shook hundreds of hands and smiled for candids, while Prince Andrew stood there a trifle out of sorts. Hollywood royalty outpoints Windsor royalty!

"And better brand recognition, at least in America. I had an impulse to lean over to His Highness, as we had been told to address him, and ask, 'So how was it with Koo Stark?' But I didn't."

Well, he might have gone stark raving mad (pardon the pun), or perhaps shrugged it off as an embarrassingly bad day. Such are the perils that come with personality when one becomes commodified. It has become a truism that if you value your privacy, you shouldn't be a celebrity. Why the needless anxiety over whether people are going to shake your hand or not, or whether your sex life becomes fodder for the gossip columns? One becomes a brand only if one chooses to be, after all, and one duly pays the price.

Robert Redford once illustrated this in an *Esquire* magazine profile. A woman saw him in public, and she asked him if he was indeed Robert Redford. "Only when I'm by myself," Redford replied. There spoke someone who could assert his place, because he knew how and when to express his branding.

Jordan Raphael

Jordan Raphael is the co-author of *Stan Lee and the Rise and Fall of the American Comic Book*, a study of the life of the creator of Spider-man and other comic-book heroes, published by Chicago Review Press in 2003. He received his Master of Arts in Journalism in 2001 from the University of Southern California, and is a reporter with the *Los Angeles Times*. The book arose from a piece he wrote on Stan Lee, for the weekend *Los Angeles Times Magazine*.

When you worked on your book, were you aware of Stan Lee's celebrity status beyond the world of comic books or was that not of concern to you?

I was. His celebrity and status relative to those of his co-creators, like Jack Kirby and Steve Ditko, were elements that interested me. Specifically, why was he so famous while other artists were relatively unknown in the world at large? I think he's seen by the public as a genial figure, charming and enthusiastic. If anything, I think his celebrity – the intensity and durability of it – nearly dwarfs his accomplishments. He hasn't actively written or edited comic books since 1972, and he's still the go-to person for most newspaper and magazine articles about comic books. It's an odd phenomenon.

Do you think comic book writers have a legitimate place in the culture of celebrity worship today?

Yes, at least as legitimate as anyone else, including screenwriters, producers, lawyers, or racehorses.

How would you say comic books have influenced or inspired you personally?

When I was a kid, I was a huge comic-book nut. That continued through my teens, when I worked at a comic-book shop, and well into college, where I published a comic-book anthology and worked for the trade magazine the *Comics Journal*. When I became a journalist, I took every opportunity to write about comics in mainstream venues because I felt it was sort of a mission to spread the gospel about this wonderful yet under-appreciated art form. Personally, I think comics have helped keep me young. On the other hand, they might have reduced my attention span and patience for longer works.

What is your own honest opinion of Spider-Man 2, *the movie?*

It was really terrific. It's been successful because people love Spider-Man and he's been translated more than amazingly to the big screen through the awesome talents of director Sam Raimi. There have only been three major superheroes in the 20th century – Superman, Batman, and Spider-man.

I once interviewed someone who told me she was thrilled when she once met Christopher Reeve because she "finally met Superman." Can you relate to this or do you think she's being silly?

She's being silly. Actually, I don't go in for that kind of parasocial behavior. I think if I actually met Superman – you know, the real Kryptonian in a blue-and-red costume – I would be thrilled. But the dudes who have portrayed him on TV and in film were not as cool.

Have you ever purchased anything because of a celebrity?

Is the Berlin Wall a celebrity? When I was 16 years old, I bought a piece of the Berlin Wall for US$20. It was probably fake, though.

3
Rock and a Hard Place: Celebrity and Music

It began from a single yet overwhelmingly historic confluence of events: Rock music saw light of day at the same time that television arrived in American homes.

That was the summer of 1954, when a young truck driver from Tupelo, Mississippi named Elvis Presley recorded the album that would change history forever: *The Sun Sessions*. We can now look back on this with wonderment, and marvel over the sheer impact of television, and the events that paved the way: The day the Beatles appeared on the *Ed Sullivan Show*; the time Elvis appeared and they had to shoot him only from the waist up, lest impressionable teenagers think lewd thoughts; the day John Lennon died.

Music is an aural art form that offers sublime pleasures unlike any other medium, and its idols become icons in ways unlike any other area of human endeavor. Marketing experts call this "ingredient branding" – in much the same way as say Compaq computers carry the "Intel Inside" logo, so that the "house brand" and its "special ingredient" form a perfect symbiosis.

Many music icons, who have become brands because they are household names, are unique in their "special ingredient" quotient. Jimi Hendrix and Carlos Santana, for instance, are excellent examples; both have guitar-playing styles that are instantly identifiable. Others have done so by achieving notoriety; singer/pianist Jerry Lee Lewis, an early rock rebel with an already-colorful love life, was arrested in November 1976 for brandishing a pistol outside Graceland and demanding to see Elvis, while the late Janis Joplin was once arrested, as was often the case, on two counts of using vulgar and indecent language, found guilty in absentia and fined US$200 – a trifle in the Joplin scandal canon. The Doors lead singer Jim Morrison was busted for public indecency in Florida, and died amid some controversy. The list goes on.

We are drawn to this tableau, this devil-may-care train wreck behavior, because the music we grew up with made nonconformity and rebellion "cool." We have accordingly spent hard-earned money on the manifestations of such "coolness," and this has accounted for the massive explosion that the concert industry has enjoyed in recent years – with tours by the likes of the Eagles, Pink Floyd, the Grateful

Dead and the Rolling Stones scoring the highest grosses at the box office.

Who would have thought that something sublime could emerge from the borderline ridiculous, as in the case of what happened in the UK in March 2003, which I mentioned in the opening chapter of this book. *Yahoo!* decided to poll 1,000 Internet users to ask them which British person, hypothetically, should best represent Earth to aliens. The winner was none other than Ozzy Osbourne, lead singer of heavy metal pioneers Black Sabbath, who took 26 percent of the vote. Internet users are a particularly media-savvy lot, attuned to the whims and fancies of modern popular culture, and they were telling the world what most music fans and rock critics already knew: You might abhor the voice (since what Ozzy does isn't always correctly called singing), but you have to admire the legend.

Ozzy Osbourne possesses a personal brand that underscores why people are so drawn to celebrities. By not pretending to be anything other than himself, he ripped asunder the veil of persona, and therein lies the real reason behind the success of his reality television series, *The Osbournes*, which depicted a family man beset by inner demons. The vicarious thrill his kind of angst has engendered is perhaps more acutely suited to rock musicians, but it also chalks up big numbers in a world inundated with broken lives made palatable for public consumption.

His life then, in a nutshell: John Michael Osbourne, from the working-class district of Aston in Birmingham, England, started out in music at age 20, and by age 54 had sold 170 million records, amassed a fortune estimated at around £30 million and now lives in a mansion in Beverly Hills, California. He has had five children by two wives; his eldest daughter Jessica, 30, and her mother, his first wife Thelma, no longer speak to him. At the end of 2002, he told writer Will Storr of *Loaded* magazine that really believes himself "mentally unbalanced – I've done so many drugs in my life that I've screwed up my brain somewhere."

So why should we sympathize with him? Because he's the real deal. There were episodes of *The Osbournes*, for instance, when he is seen pondering heavy issues like family violence. After separating his current wife Sharon and their daughter Kelly from a fight (after Kelly had thrown a bowl of hot soup over her sister Aimee), he sat and mused aloud over the sheer irony of his telling his own family about the dangers of violence. "Who the hell am I to tell them about violence?" asked this once-convicted burglar and former abattoir worker. To this day, he has never completely come to terms with his alcoholism, especially after spending a night in jail in 1989 when he was arrested for trying to kill Sharon.

He claimed no memory of the incident. "Everybody says, 'Ozzy, you're a legend' but behind the facade is a sad, lonely, wet fart of a person trying to find an excuse," he said (in the abovementioned *Loaded* interview). "I mean, for hell's sake, man, arrested for attempted murder? That ain't a very good thing."

That statement alone makes for powerful branding, since few celebrities can even come close to his track record. Ozzy's biggest claim to fame remains biting off the head of a bat at a show in Des Moines, Iowa in 1981, and he was famously jailed and banned from the state of Texas in February 1982 after he'd urinated on the Alamo state monument. In 1986, the parents of a California teenager sued Ozzy, alleging that his song "Suicide Solution" had driven the boy to kill himself. (The judge dismissed the suit; all this and more can be found in a cover story on Ozzy in *Rolling Stone*, July 25, 2002.) Finally, in an ironic twist, Ozzy's son Jack was checked into drug rehab in the summer of 2003, and so the once-wild father was now the sober one. What's not to like about that?

After all, music celebrities have always possessed a singularly gigantic advantage over those in other creative fields: Fact doesn't always have to be separate from fiction, and indeed the closer the two mesh, the better the outcome.

Myth information

How did Alanis Morissette come out of nowhere back in 1995, to sell an astonishing 14 million albums of *Jagged Little Pill*, her major-label debut album? That was a milestone for a previously unknown artist (she'd had two previous albums out, but only in her native Canada).

Four albums later, her songs still don't always sound like overtly radio-friendly pop hits, but word had certainly gotten out about her risqué subject matter. Her song "You Oughta Know" recalled her performing oral sex on a boyfriend in a movie theatre. More recently, on her 2002 album *Under Rug Swept*, "Hands Clean" discussed the perils of jailbait, based on her relationship with an older man when she was 14. She certainly knew how to jolt the jaded masses.

The way music publicity works, one would have hardly guessed the ferocity of the outcome. Usually, when an artist is signed to a record company, a writer is assigned the task of interviewing him or her and then writing the official artist "bio" (short for "biography"). This gets sent out with advance copies of the record to reviewers at the newspapers and magazines, with the idea of securing maximum press coverage.

Morissette's bio for her landmark album *Jagged Little Pill* aimed to set the tone: "To those who think the generation that came of age in the 1980s lacks focus, here's one bit of advice ... take a pill. A *Jagged Little Pill*. Although she only recently passed her 20th birthday, Alanis Morissette's Maverick debut proves she possesses a wealth of insight and an off-kilter sense of humor that's at once untainted and mature.... " (Maverick, while a nice and intended pun, actually referred to her record label, the Maverick Recording Company, owned by Madonna and distributed by Warner Bros.)

Publicity bios are marketing devices, always penned to prove a point – that the artist's own life (or unique perspective on life) can itself be a legitimate selling point. The product then goes out to the wider world on a wing and a prayer, in the hope that people will listen and agree with her "wealth of insight" and "off-kilter sense of humor," even if it's not always easy to discern what is deemed "untainted and mature."

But that's the risk, a daring gambit, in an already overcrowded marketplace where the battle rages on – to find new artists capable of rising about the fray, so that icon status can be conferred upon the chosen few.

A good publicist, however, accepts the attendant risks and rises to the challenge. One such publicist is Ronnie Lippin, who had guided the American success of Eric Clapton and who rode the crest of a wave in 2004 with her newest client, Prince. The funk-rock singer/guitarist could always be counted on to court controversy, wherever it could prove useful and profitable to him. He had famously battled with his former record label, Warner Bros., having changed his name to an unpronounceable glyph in 1993 before changing it back. On *Musicology*, his first release since 1999 and dubbed his "comeback" album of 2004, he wryly reminded everyone where he stood on the matter, even when he was now armed with a new contract with Sony Music: "Who's pimping who when nobody gets a second chance? This is the story of illusion, coma, pimp and circumstance."

This time, Prince embarked on a new ploy to re-establish himself as a brand separate from the rest. For his 63-city *Musicology* tour of North America, concertgoers were given copies of the new album as part of the price of the ticket. "Once the ticket is sold, the CD is sold," Prince himself explained to the *New York Times*. "It's one-stop shopping."

It seemed like a crazy idea, but he was proved right. Ticket-linked albums accounted for 27 percent of the album's total sales, and during the week of July 4, 2004, the album still sold 61,000 copies and stayed at number 15 on the *Billboard* albums chart even though Prince played no concerts that week. Then something even more interesting happened. Complaints were made, charging that Prince was unfairly winning by giving the album away. *Billboard* (the trade magazine that lists the charts) and SoundScan (the company that compiles the sales figures for the charts) then changed the method for counting album sales.

This was astounding – who'd have thought one man could change the way record sales are tabulated? Now, if an album was sold with a concert ticket, the buyer had to specifically authorize a surcharge for the price of the album for the sale to be counted. However, the rule was not retroactive, which meant that Prince continued his ride near the top of the charts for as long as he remained on tour. He had launched a pre-emptive strike. In this age of rampant online downloads and illegal file-sharing, getting some-one to actually buy your CD can be a near-impossible task, but Prince found a smart way around it.

He'd also selectively chosen a few public appearances to announce his return to performing. In April 2004, he played to more than 19,000 people at the Staples Center in Los Angeles, a record for that arena, and he also performed a memorable duet with the R&B diva Beyoncé at the Grammy awards. Additionally, he announced that he would play some of his old favorites for the very last time on this tour, an old trick but it helped sell out six arena shows in the New York area and five in Southern California. Online sales for the *Musicology* album were also reserved for his own website, where his fans could download the entire album for a mere US$9.99. (The CD retailed at US$18.99.)

In an interview for this book (done with her full consent, even though major entertainment publicists rarely give interviews), Ronnie Lippin disclosed that she had never represented Prince before and saw him as a new challenge, a welcome addition to her already stellar client list – virtually a who's who in popular music: the Bee Gees, the Who, Eric Clapton, Peter Frampton, Brian Wilson, Mark Knopfler, Michael McDonald, Johnny Mathis, Lynyrd Skynyrd, and more.

"Prince was looking for new representation and asked someone in the industry for referrals," she explained. "Prince and I then spoke on the phone and he decided on that first phone call to hire me. I had no reservations whatsoever. I was honored that someone of his talent was willing to allow me to interface with the media and, ultimately, with his audiences." The decision to tie the CD sales to the ticket sales, she reveals, was Prince's. Her job was to "position" this to the media and the public.

Strategy and stealth

The usual routine, for most publicists, is to find the best media outlets for the artist – usually print (magazines and newspapers) and television (talk shows) – but with Prince, Lippin took a strategic tack.

"There are always certain outlets that are on a wish list – generally those with the biggest audiences – but Prince is a very interesting performer with a unique point of view, so we took a different route," Lippin recalled. "For example, his first national TV appearance was on PBS's *Tavis Smiley Show*. Prince had the full half hour and did a wonderful acoustic performance. This was broadcast before all the other television appearances he did – *The Tonight Show with Jay Leno*, *The Today Show*, and more. He also did interviews on CNBC and on CNNfn. I secured magazine covers for him in a number of outlets ranging from *Rolling Stone, Entertainment Weekly* and *Guitar Player* to his hometown *Minneapolis Saint Paul* city magazine."

Lippin had created a snowball effect, whereby Prince could be seen as making a "comeback" initially in smaller, less obvious media outlets that were not necessarily music-related. (Tavis Smiley is an African-American talk show host, and his public television program is sponsored by the retail giant Wal-Mart.) The bottom line, for Lippin, was that "Prince is open to suggestions" even while he remained the final arbiter of the given choices.

"Any artist or celebrity who is in the news media works hard for the media's – and the public's – attention and trust," she added. "This is not a casual process but a creative effort, combined with planning. With Prince, he is the one delivering not only the music but also the final decisions about his business and public image, so he is very much involved in what is going on in his career. It is my responsibility to stay ahead of the curve but the decision to proceed or not always rests in Prince's hands."

Given her track record of creating branding for so many music celebrities, does she feel she has a special perspective to share about working with such luminaries? "Interesting question!" she replied. "I am often amazed – and amused – that I seem to work well with major artists, and I attribute it to my Brooklyn public school background. Although I certainly moved on after high school – I went to college and got my degree and traveled – I still see things from a very grounded perspective. I am *not* the celebrities I represent, nor do I want to be them. I have a very defined role for them.

"My job is to analyze their public image and figure out how to position them and their products in front of audiences that are likely to be receptive. I never buy into the 'any publicity is good publicity' theory. My job is to help them generate only positive coverage."

"These are people," she matter-of-factly noted of her clients. "They have moods. They have emotions. They have families and they have careers. The only difference is that their careers place them in front of a very large audience."

Even in far-flung places like the Far East, Prince has proved a crowd magnet and a CD mega-seller. "The new record has done pretty well for us in Hong Kong, and I think one of the main reasons is because he played at the Harbourfest in 2003," said Hong Kong-based Kieven Yim, Sony BMG Music Entertainment's director of strategic marketing in Asia. Prince opened the festival, aimed at attracting people to Hong Kong in the wake of the SARS epidemic, which also featured the Gypsy Kings, Santana, and Neil Young.

"It was a full house – 30,000 people turned up to see Prince! – and it was a fantastic gig. This was in October 2003 – *Musicology* hadn't come out yet, it was released in April 2004 – and, in fact, he wasn't even signed to us at that point. So he didn't do any press interviews for us when he was here. Nobody was really marketing him at the time.

"I think Harbourfest had a part to play in his current success, without a doubt. When we shipped, the album went gold – that's 10,000 copies, in Hong Kong – and then it's a matter of getting the momentum going. I'm not surprised. I think it's one of his best records for a long, long time, and I'm not just saying that."

Ticket prices for major acts, even from a supposedly bygone era, remain steep but sell steadily. People still pay good money for their celebrity brands. This is largely due, in my own opinion, to the fact that scarcity drives demand – major music acts seldom tour in Asia unless they are committed to playing dates in Japan (the world's second biggest music market, after the United States) and agree to swing through en route to Australia. Promoters pay astronomical fees to bring them out, and so they have to charge exorbitant prices to recoup costs.

There is also a "be there or be square" factor, as those who can afford the ticket prices are ever willing to pay top dollar for bragging rights – and to look cool themselves, because they were seen out in public at a cool event. In recent years, when the Rolling Stones and David Bowie played in Hong Kong, the top prices were in the region of US$256 (about HK$2,000). Bowie played one show to a near-capacity crowd. The Stones played two shows and sold out both.

David Bowie, in point of fact, shares a crucial similarity with Prince. He has always been a man on a mission, an *agent provocateur*, someone who goes the extra mile to provoke social tension. Where Prince used the power of human sexuality, Bowie relied on devices charged with more abstract yet equally socially galvanizing symbolism. Many of his fans discovered his music during the early 1970s, when he wore a dress and held the torch for androgyny, even openly declaring his bisexuality at a time when no other major artists dared to do so. When I met him in 1995 and asked him whether he'd ever been plagued by doubts about alienating his listeners, he matter-of-factly replied that he didn't much care.

"I'm completely and absolutely indifferent to that," he told me. "It's of absolutely no interest to me what one person in Croydon might feel. I think that the moments that I have conceived of writing for other people have been generally the most artistically disappointing moments that I've worked in. I work at my best when I'm writing completely and only for my own expression. When I've done that, then my presumption is that if I enjoy something then there has to be somebody out there, to a lesser or greater degree, who will also enjoy it. Now, that audience will go up and down vastly, depending on the nature of the work, but there will always be somebody somewhere who will identify with what I'm doing. And I know that's my territory. I have to take into account that my audience will always be vacillating backwards and forwards between great interest and virtually no interest at all. But that comes with the territory, if I'm going to work this way."

Creating culthood

So much has been written about David Bowie, yet one of the very best and most insightful pieces never saw the light of day. Steve Turner's article, "How to Become a Cult Figure in Only Two Years: The Making of David Bowie," a previously unpublished 1974 piece commissioned by the defunct British magazine, *Nova* (now published on the Rock's Back Pages online music archive, at www.rocksbackpages.com) posed a relevant point: "How is it possible to make something extraordinary of an ordinary member of the public? The point is, you don't have to. It's not the person you have to change, it's the public perception of the person."

David Bowie embarked on his music career fully aware of this. In 1971 he told the *Cheltenham Chronicle*, "I believe in fantasy and star images. I am very aware of these kinds of people and feel they are important figures in our society. People like to focus on somebody who they might consider not quite the same as them. Whether it's true or not is immaterial." This is echoed by Brian Ward, the photographer responsible for the covers of Bowie's first two albums on the RCA label. "He [Bowie] knows exactly where he's going. He always comes to you with a definite idea of what he wants but he also respects what you're doing and leaves you a lot of room to work."

For the *Hunky Dory* (1971) album cover, Bowie arrived at Ward's studio with a book on Marlene Dietrich and pointed out a particular photograph he wanted imitated. For the more famous *Ziggy Stardust* album (*The Rise and Fall of Ziggy Stardust and the Spiders from Mars*, released in 1972), he asked Ward to check out a location for what he described as "a Brooklyn alley scene" where he'd appear alone like some alien being. "He was playing with this man-from-Mars thing," recalls Ward. "He wanted to come over like a real stranger, like something out of a science-fiction movie."

The reference is telling, since Bowie then played a Martian in the film *The Man Who Fell to Earth*, based on the classic Robert Heinlein science fiction novel *Stranger in a Strange Land*. His first big hit, "Space Oddity," recorded in 1969, was inspired by Stanley Kubrick's film *2001: A Space Odyssey*, but its real stroke of brilliance lay in the timing; it was released to coincide with the first American manned moon landing on July 20, 1969. Much of Bowie's early success relied on such shrewd marketing and publicity. Steve Turner noted the input of Mick Rock, the photographer hired to shoot Bowie's early concerts. Only those of Rock's images considered suitable for publication, by Bowie and his then-manager Tony DeFries, were used. (Of late, Rock has published a lavish coffee-table book devoted to photos of yet another iconic act, Debbie Harry and her band Blondie.) Bowie, always a voracious reader, drew many ideas about his own imagery from books like *The Hidden Persuaders* by Vance Packard and *The Neophiliacs* by Christopher Booker.

"The essence of fantasy is that it feeds on a succession of unresolved images," wrote Booker, "each of which arouses anticipation, leading to the demand for a new image to be put in its place. All fantasy images excite the mind by the fact that they are incomplete and cannot be properly resolved.

"They tantalise and egg on the imagination in the same way as an object only seen indistinctly, because it does not provide the brain with sufficient information to clearly make it out, may tease and excite our minds into thinking it larger and more awesome than it in fact is."

Bowie brought this to life by carefully managing his public persona. He gave very few interviews, so as to create a sense of rarity that could be prized. (Tony Visconti, his former bass guitarist and record producer, explained it simply in the *Nova* article: "He's very aware of the mystery he's created and he's keen to keep it that way.") And when he did grant interviews, he could be aptly cryptic, like when he told *Rolling Stone* magazine, "I don't feel I'm a person at all sometimes. I'm just a collection of other people's ideas."

By creating stage personas with bizarre names like Ziggy Stardust, Aladdin Sane, and the Thin White Duke, Bowie milked this to the max. When he did give interviews, he was solicitous and deferential with the forthright charm of an English gentleman, and when he didn't want to talk he simply didn't. He must have known that, in due time, his place in the annals of pop culture would be secure. In such manner, Bowie has escaped the straitjacket that has been the bane of so many young artists, people who score big hits early in their careers only to fall into obscurity as they grow up.

Tiffany, who once ruled American radio with her hits "I Think We're Alone Now" and "I Saw Him Standing There" (from her self-titled debut album of 1987, which sold four million copies) now sees the irony in the title of another of her hits, "Could've Been." In an interview accompanying a nude photo spread in *Playboy*, April 2002, timed to support her latest comeback album *The Color of Silence*, she reflected: "I was on tour in the late Eighties and noticed that music was changing, becoming more R&B and dance-oriented .... It became very frustrating for me as a young adult because people saw me as the sweet and innocent girl next door. I knew my peers were growing up – girls wanted to look sexier, and I didn't know how to make that transition." *The Color of Silence* bombed; evidently, not enough people cared to hear a grown-up Tiffany sing well-crafted ballads about grown-up issues.

Tiffany's arch-rival Debbie Gibson also found herself falling into the same quandary but bounced back by effectively "rebranding" herself as a Broadway singer – she gained newfound fame and acclaim as Eponine in the Broadway production of *Les Misérables* and then Sandy in the London production of *Grease*. She also formed her own record label, Golden Egg Records, which released her most recent, 2001 pop album, *M.Y.O.B.* ("Mind Your Own Business," itself a sarcastic stab at the mainstream pop media for ignoring her). The rebranding exercise became complete with the continued use of her new name, Deborah (and no longer the teenage-sounding Debbie) Gibson. She had successfully rebranded herself by imposing a new "value proposition" – a new product for a new price.

This is no mean feat, particularly in a world already overcrowded with female singer/songwriters. For every Sheryl Crow who gets to be cited in *In Style* magazine for her fashion fabulousness (Dolce & Gabbana, Yves Saint Laurent, Bottega Veneta, Robert Clergerie), there are a thousand others who never make the cut. How do we explain the megastar status of "country" singers like Faith Hill and

Shania Twain? Or the fact that Kylie Minogue was voted the female celebrity with the best legs in a 2004 survey conducted by the razor company Gillette (the runners-up were Cameron Diaz, Nicole Kidman, Anna Kournikova, and Kate Moss) while her sister, Dannii Minogue, continues to struggle with her career, despite the fact that both sisters deal in the same frothy dance-pop genre?

Some of this can obviously be attributed to the influence of MTV. "People attach a fetish value to records and videos," said Robert Vianello, from the Department of Communication Studies at California State University, Los Angeles (when I interviewed him in 1985, for a monograph I was then writing about the effects of music video). "It's a perversion of art, though I'm not sure video producers see what they do as art because the bottom line is to sell the group featured in the video."

The list of acts that have sold millions of albums, almost purely on the strength of high-rotation video play, is long. Mariah Carey, Sade, and Enya come readily to mind. Enya, the Irish singer/ keyboardist who made Celtic music safe for the masses (with tunes inspired by the Catholic mass, no less), sold an astonishing 17 million CDs – the combined worldwide sales of her two break-through albums, 1988's *Watermark* and 1991's *Shepherd Moons* – despite playing no concerts at all until 2001 (unless one counts a single American television performance on *The Tonight Show with Jay Leno*).

Led Zeppelin, who peaked in the mid-1970s, never had that luxury; music videos didn't exist back then. What Zeppelin had in common with Enya, however, was perfect timing.

"To have been white and male and 16 or 17 in America as the 1960s blurred and darkened into the '70s was to have sensed, amid the generalized tumult, a singularly deafening commotion: Led Zeppelin was in the neighborhood," recalled Gerald Marzorati in the *New York Times* in May 2003, a piece announcing the new concert-footage *Led Zeppelin DVD* release. "This had something to do with FM radio, which was no longer underground but widespread, successful and as eager as Top 40 stations had been in their heyday to promote the next new thing, which Led Zeppelin represented. And

71

this also had something to do with the new dashboard-mounted, eight-track tape deck, for which Led Zeppelin's music was perfectly suited."

This was aided by osmosis, the kind which Led Zeppelin (and other major acts of that time, like Steely Dan and the Eagles) had managed to drum into public consciousness, thanks in large part to American FM radio. That's how they all became household names. Enya, on the other hand, arrived on the scene just as a newer technology – compact discs – was taking off. Her music, with its shimmering sonic gloss and multi-tracked layers of vocals and keyboards, was perfectly suited to the audiophile quality of CDs.

Something can surely be said, then, for reaching the largest number of people at the most opportune time. Legends are born that way.

The same applied to the US Presidential election of 1992, which some social scientists believe was actually won five months before the votes were in. It all happened on the night the Democrat challenger Bill Clinton performed on television, on the *Arsenio Hall Show*, blowing a mean saxophone and looking very much the personification of cool. So many bought the package because they bought his brand, and they ushered him into the White House where they hoped he would swing the country to a new groove.

America has always acted on its spiritual legacy of renewed optimism, born of post-colonial independence, and has always rewarded well those perceived to be heroes. Even today, the playing field is uneven; certain recording superstars enjoy a higher "enhanced artist" royalty rate for CD sales. Big-name "superstars" will get paid 28.5 percent or more, whereas most others on the roster will receive about 26.7 percent, off the "PPD" (the wholesale "Purchase Price to Dealers," not the retail price). The figures themselves vary, according to artist and record company.

Some might ask if they deserve this. The real question, really, is why they have been elevated to such esteemed status. We want our heroes so badly, it would appear, that we are willing to grant them special standing, since they can achieve sales levels commensurate with their status.

Hence, titles of lofty grandeur are conferred, however subjective the perception. Some celebrities handle this sort of thing better than others, because they know their own branding. "How do you feel about *Vogue* magazine calling you 'the Mariah Carey of folk'?" I once asked the Alaskan folk-pop songbird Jewel Kilcher, better known to all as just Jewel. "I don't know," she replied. "Ask Mariah Carey."

Ronnie Lippin

Ronnie Lippin is a veteran music publicist, who has represented Eric Clapton, Peter Frampton, Mark Knopfler, Brian Wilson, Johnny Mathis, Michael McDonald, the Who, and Lynyrd Skynyrd. In 2004, she shepherded the much-lauded comeback of the soul-funk legend Prince. She is president of The Lippin Group, with offices in Los Angeles, New York, and London.

How did Prince come to you as a client? Had you represented him before?

No, I had never had the pleasure of representing him before. He had been looking for new representation and asked someone in the industry for referrals. Prince and I spoke on the phone and he decided on that first phone call to hire me. I had no reservations whatsoever about accepting. I am honored that someone of his talent was willing to allow me to interface with the media and, ultimately, with his audiences.

Did you help to strategize the whole campaign whereby his ticket sales were tied to album sales?

Prince made the decision to tie the CD in with the ticket price. My job was, and is, to position that to the media and the public.

Were there any particular avenues that you used for him that might be out of the norm or unique?

There are always certain media outlets that are on a wish list, and these are generally those with the biggest audiences. But Prince is a very interesting performer with a unique point of view, so we took a different route. For example, his first national television appearance was on public television, on PBS's *Tavis Smiley Show*. Prince had the full half-hour and did a wonderful acoustic performance. This was broadcast before he did *The Tonight Show With Jay Leno* and *The Today Show*, and the rest. He also did interviews on CNBC and CNNfn, and I secured magazine covers for him in a number of outlets ranging from *Rolling Stone* and *Entertainment Weekly* to *Guitar Player* and his hometown *Minneapolis Saint Paul* city magazine.

You were quoted in the Wall Street Journal *as saying that a comeback like Prince's "doesn't just happen. It is far from a casual process, and Prince is the primary force driving everything." Can you elaborate?*

The bottom line is that Prince is open to suggestions. Any artist or celebrity who is in the news works hard for the media's and the public's attention and trust. Prince delivers in his concerts and on his CDs, and he has done so for decades, but this is not a casual process. It is a creative effort combined with planning. Prince is the one delivering not only the music but also the final decisions about his business and public image. He is very much involved in what is going on in his career. It is my responsibility to stay ahead of the curve but the decision to proceed or not always rests in his hands.

You've had a long track record of handling many superstar careers, which leads to the inference that you are unfazed by celebrity.

My clients are people. They have moods, they have emotions, they have families, and they have careers. The only difference is that their careers place them in front of a very large audience.

Do you believe that you might have some kind of special perspective, that equips you to work well with such celebrities?

Interesting question! I am often amazed – and amused – that I seem to work well with major artists. I attribute this to my Brooklyn public school background. I see things from a very grounded perspective. I am not the celebrities I represent, nor do I want to be them. I have a very defined role for them. My job is to analyze their public image and figure out how to position them and their products in front of audiences that are likely to be receptive. I never buy into the "any publicity is good publicity" theory. My job is to help generate only positive coverage. I stay very focused.

Has there been a celebrity that stands out in your long list of past clients as being particularly memorable to work with, and why?

Yes. Johnny Mathis. I had just arrived in Los Angeles and was driving a borrowed car, a real clunker. I had to pick up Mathis and take him to a very big media event. We arrived unnoticed. But when the event was over, everyone lined up for the valet at the same time. When my jalopy was brought to the door, one of the executives at the agency where I was working rushed up. He said to Mathis that he could not step into that car without embarrassing himself. Mathis told him: "Ronnie brought me here, and I'm going back home with her." And he did.

4
Rags to Riches: Celebrity and Fashion

"One should either be a work of art, or wear a work of art," Oscar Wilde observed, in *Phrases and Philosophies for the Use of the Young*. Such was the subtext very much at work when Britney Spears famously strode onto a Milan runway in October 2002, clad in a rainbow-spangled gown by Donatella Versace costing a mere US$23,000 – small change, presumably, for someone whose break-through album, *Oops ... I Did It Again*, had entered the *Billboard* chart at number one and sold 1.319 million copies in its first week back in May 2000, an all-time record for a female artist.

The very essence of glamour is to invoke envy, after all. This is the same prevailing reason that the tabloids continued to point their barbed telescopes on Britney's antithesis, the she-devil rock star Courtney Love, who once charmed the cameras with her own Versace moment, striding down the red carpet at Cannes when she was promoting her scene-stealing role in *The People Versus Larry Flynt*. Love has perfected the art of appearing oblivious to criti-cism, particularly about her ongoing drug-rehab psychodramas (including defending her use of Vicodin as "the new LSD – 'Lead Singer's Drug'" – according to the celebrity gossip website *Popbitch*, on July 23, 2004). She had also appeared on the cover of *Allure* magazine, decked out in Gucci and offering, in the interview inside, details of her adventures in plastic surgery. Her red patent-leather mules were by Marc Jacobs, and her daughter Frances Bean wore platform Skechers (perhaps influenced by Britney Spears's Skechers ads).

The hallowed place that *Allure* once occupied has since been usurped by *In Style* magazine, devoted to the celebrity lifestyle in relation to fashion and other finery. "We were the first magazine to show a celebrity on the red carpet from head to toe, so that readers could see that aside from the gown, what handbag, what shoes and even what toe polish color she is wearing," said Kim-Van Dang, beauty director of *In Style*, from her office in New York. "It seems simple, but that concept didn't exist until *In Style* created it."

"The style in *In Style* goes beyond the outfits. It's really the first celebrity lifestyle magazine, where readers get to learn not just what's in a star's closet, but what kind of face cream she favors, why she dyed her hair or cut it short and how she feels about the change, what her home is like, who her gal pals are, whether she loves dogs or cats or both, where she got that great lamp, which philanthropic causes she cares deeply about, what her favorite dish to cook is, along with the family recipe."

One of *In Style*'s consistently brilliant tactics has been to offer fashion advice within the context of celebrity culture, by showcasing what the stars wore on movie sets or at home. "*In Style* shows celebrities not simply as beautiful, rich, and famous, but as real people that real people can relate to," Dang added, almost stating the obvious. "I like to say that *In Style* is a how-to service book disguised as a glam, glossy one." More cynical readers might sneer at, say, Christy Turlington and her line of yoga clothing. "I don't think celebrities need to justify what they endorse," Dang noted. "It's their business. They choose their affiliations wisely and use the top stylists and photographers in these campaigns. I can't think of an instance when their celebrity image has been compromised."

In the mood for style

The larger idea is to create a palpable sense of aspiration – that you, as a consumer, can enhance your own "personal brand" by way of say, an article entitled "Asset Management" ("Tips on making the most of your figure" using Calvin Klein's latest summer shades) in the magazine's "Stylefile" section. "Women are inspired by what they see everywhere they see it," Dang declared. "From the screen to the street to the beach. The economy influences fashion, as do the Olympics, the War on Terror, and, of course, what we're showing in this month's issue of *In Style*!" Dang herself has participated in the style-making fun; in the September 1999 issue of the magazine, she was photographed with actress Mariska Hargitay (the youngest daughter of screen siren Jayne Mansfield and Emmy Award-winning star of the television series *Law & Order: Special Victims Unit*), in which they "were up all night on location in NYC, where they shared date make-up tips."

Popular culture, Dang observed, is an arbiter of fashion-forward taste. "Take, for instance, the way the West Coast is now having a resurgence – witness the recent interest in surfing culture," she said when interviewed for this book in the summer of 2004. "Even Chanel designed a surf-inspired collection – and a surfboard! That said, *uber*-popular shows shot in New York City like *Sex and the City* certainly get women across the country to dress up. In the end, a woman likes what she likes. Silhouettes that look good on her body type. Colors that complement her hair, eye, and skin tones. Style that expresses her personality and that works for her lifestyle. She might idolize a certain celebrity, but she will wear what makes her comfortable, be it a pair of flats or stilettos."

Movies, of course, have always reflected fashion trends, though Dang expressed skepticism about the extent of their influence. For his fall 2004 ads for Yves Saint Laurent, creative director Doug Lloyd was inspired by the Hong Kong film *In the Mood for Love*, starring Tony Leung and Maggie Cheung as repressed lovers in 1950s Shang-hai. "A more romantic feel," Lloyd disclosed, "less overtly sexual in nature. That's the direction fashion is going in right now.... It's all about grooming, with a polish modeled on old Hollywood glamour."

But that, Dang countered, is only half the equation. "Sex – overt or not – always sells," she noted. "Even as this year's fall clothing gets more conservative in nature, the hair and make-up direction is getting wilder. Hair for fall is more textured, more mussed, almost fuzzy in feeling, and black eyeliner has taken a life of its own, as has the liberal use is bright and bold and metallic colors for eyes, lips and cheeks. It's a game of balance."

Celebrities constantly deal with this game of balance. "They have their fair share of hair-disaster stories, skincare issues, and make-up obsessions, just like the rest of us," Dang observed. "Some celebrities have great taste. Others have great stylists."

Naturally, *In Style* has always devoted much space to these stylists. Federic Fekkai talked about the "sexy but romantic" looks he created for the likes of Salma Hayek, Linda Fiorentino, and Cate Blanchett. Larry Waggoner revealed how he styled Ashley Judd. Elsewhere, in countless other magazines, a battery of beauty experts have told all in pithy quotes: "Base coat is the most important ingredient for any manicure," said Kate Moss's manicurist, Leighton Denny; "The perfect cut can change your life," said Elizabeth Hurley's hairdresser, Richard Ward.

Magazine editors naturally love this sort of thing, since it feeds the omnipresent market for fashion tips, as culled from lives of the rich and famous. Women surely want to know how a rock star like Gwen Stefani got all dolled-up to play Jean Harlow in the film *The Aviator*. Brad Pitt and George Clooney are suddenly credited with the return to fashion of the Trilby hat. And what variation of the Humphrey Bogart trenchcoat was featured yet again, in another recapitulation of recommended menswear? Even tennis star Serena Williams, a self-confessed aspiring actress, has her own clothing line now, called Aneres ("Serena" spelled backwards).

The choices are endless, the possibilities ever-percolating, and they emphasize a truism: Clothes and shoes, scents and sensibilities, they're all about encasing a person in garments that serve to make a statement – that you are who you choose to present to the world.

In the often image-conscious world of fashion, there exists the ultimate embodiment of celebrity branding – because clothes adorn and drape the human body, what is being sold is the very sense of a person's actual being. The way a celebrity will pout insouciantly or nod nonchalantly in a photograph makes a statement that inevitably sells products. That's what we buy into when perfumes and apparel become part of a diva's "brand extension" – Jennifer Lopez is a good example, with her perfumes Glow and Still – and also what we are forced to ponder when certain supermodels issue political statements based on their lifestyle choice – protesting the use of fur on behalf of organizations like PETA (People for the Ethical Treatment of Animals) comes to mind.

Even Jackie Chan doesn't sell only movies any more; he has his own clothing line too. This is distinctly different from the way that, say, Brad Pitt has posed in ads selling jeans in Korea. When celebrities own the fashion brand that bears their name, the impact is far more powerful and profound. It is also provocative in terms of catalyzing lifestyle change. Yohji Yamamoto, the iconoclastic Japanese designer, once said, "If you want to wear my clothes, change your way of life."

That was his way of making a political statement, hardly a flippant one at all. Lots of time and money have been spent convincing people of this. For instance, J. Walter Thompson utilized the services of supermodel Kate Moss in an ad campaign for Rimmel cosmetics in the UK, called "Reclaiming the streets of London"; because "Kate Moss is the ultimate London girl: cool, experimental and edgy and a bit of a chameleon," explained the campaign's account director Kenny Hill, "which fits perfectly with the experimental, fun side of Rimmel."

The idea worked like a charm. In the year ending March 2002, Rimmel had a net sales increase of 21 percent and a profit jump of 25 percent. Overall, in just six months, the company had increased its profitability by 25 percent – remarkable, considering that beginning from the previous October it had decided to mark up its prices by some 14 percent from the previous year (and up by 29 percent from the previous two years), bolstered by Kate Moss's sultry stare above the ad copy ("New Sheer Temptation lipstick ... Take a fresh shine to your lips.")

Banking hopes on a single celebrity might seem foolhardy, but Rimmel's choice of Kate Moss actually palls in comparison to some others, most notably the way De Beers, the world's largest diamond producer, chose the Somalian supermodel Iman, the wife of rock star David Bowie, as its face to the world. As Hamish Pringle, in his 2004 book *Celebrity Sells*, noted: "In 2001, the diamond giant made a decisive switch from a supply control to a demand-led business model," and this led to "an excellent example where the use of a celebrity has helped create a new brand identity and positioning."

Many celebrity branding exercises are "demand-led" – they speak directly to consumers, who then dictate demand with their choices, predicated almost entirely on their popularity of the celebrity in question. Iman was chosen by De Beers's ad agency, J. Walter Thompson, because the diamonds were being sold to a younger, contemporary market. Her unique selling points were her exotic African heritage

(De Beers, a South African company, was said to be reaching back to its African roots) as well as the British Bowie cachet (De Beers was founded in 1888, during South Africa's British colonial era).

Icon and inspiration

A huge campaign was accordingly built around Iman. A mega-poster of her graced the exterior of the De Beers UK flagship office on London's Bond Street, when it opened in November 2002. This was aided and abetted by some serious numbers – because of De Beers, the marketing spend by the diamond jewelry industry now amounted to some US$180 million, double the previous year. At the end of July 2003, De Beers posted impressive results: diamond sales were up 2.75 percent (to US$2.92 billion) and profits were up 34 percent (to US$414 million), for the first half of 2003.

"I will not be a model but an icon and an inspiration," Iman told the *International Herald Tribune*, when the new jewelry brand De Beers LV (a joint venture with Louis Vuitton) was launched at the 2002 Cannes Film Festival. Iman, at the time, was also co-chair (along with Sharon Stone and Elton John) of Elizabeth Taylor's AMFAR (American Foundation for AIDS Research), and she had earlier, in 2000, brought out her own I-Iman cosmetic range, an extension of her 1994 participation with the Women of Color brand of beauty products.

Those are merely some examples of how sectors of the fashion business have gained from the choice of matching the right celebrity to the right product. The psychological lynchpin that makes it all work is often in the realm of photography. The likes of Irving Penn and the late Richard Avedon have been chosen for their ability to seduce consumers, since at their level of artistry they can create images offering a visual shorthand – the kind that instantly conveys to the consumer self-affirming notions of glamour and elegance. "Cindy Crawford's choice" (the catch-phrase of her Omega watch ads) is an almost too-blatant way to state the strategy, since the operative word here is surely "choice."

It's a brilliant conspiracy, equally brilliantly summed up by the aesthetician John Berger in his classic book *Ways of Seeing*:

> Publicity, it is thought, offers a free choice.... Publicity is not merely an assembly of competing messages: it is a language in itself which is always used to make the same general proposal. Within publicity, choices are offered between this cream and that cream, that car and this car, but publicity as a system only makes a single proposal. It proposes to each of us that we transform ourselves, or our lives, by buying something more.
>
> This more, it proposes, will make us in some way richer – even though we will be poorer for having spent our money. Publicity persuades us of such a transformation by showing us people who have apparently been transformed and are, as a result, enviable. The state of being envied is what constitutes glamour. And publicity is the process of manufacturing glamour.

Not everyone chosen to project glamour relishes the idea, even as they accept it as part and parcel of the process. Take, for instance, the pop/opera singer Emma Shapplin, who embodies all the sophistication of the modern French woman, she who wields her *je ne sais quoi* with purposeful intent. The way she glides into a public space, whether it is a press conference or a photo shoot, you might think she'd been doing it all her life. Small wonder, then, that Shapplin's publicity bio for her 2002 album *Etterna* dubbed her "the sexy French diva who has given opera sex appeal."

On the day I met with her at a photo shoot, Shapplin was clad in Ungaro: a black dress, all frilly and pleated, with shoes by Sergio Rossi and fingerless leather gloves that she'd designed, cut, and stitched herself. The Ungaro part is the most interesting, actually, since she was given the dress to wear on tour, specifically on occasions like these – so that the public will see her dressed in Ungaro.

In the jargon of fashion marketing, she is playing the role of a "prescriptor," much like Nicole Kidman has been for Chanel or

Monica Bellucci for Cartier, a visual enticement for product placement. It's a well-known, standard practice. Design houses do this
every year before the Oscars, for instance, flooding the already
bulging wardrobes of A-list stars with new frockery expressly primed
for red-carpet, photo-op appeal. (When Julia Roberts won her Best
Actress award for *Erin Brockovich*, she'd arrived in a Valentino
gown which a gasping Hilary Swank admitted she'd nearly chosen
for herself. Word of this got out, of course, leading some to ponder if
this had been a neatly planned publicity ploy on the part of
Valentino; after all, what better way to draw attention than to have
two stars coveting the same dress?)

"I don't know," Emma Shapplin murmured, when I asked her
about her unequivocally sensual images. "That's funny stuff. For me,
the visual part is very important. Even when I write music, it very
often comes with an image. I need to 'dream myself,' as I like to say,
so the visuals are always important. I could of course just put text on
my CD covers and have no photos of myself, but my manager and
my record company said no. There are a lot of photos of me inside
the CD sleeve anyway. I like to have these photos because I like to
play with characters. When I see them I don't see me. You know what
I mean? It's like I'm a character. That's what I see, without being
pretentious. Because I don't see me."

In the small print of her *Etterna* CD booklet, "wardrobe" is credited to Alberta Ferretti, Gian Franco Ferre, Gucci, Donna Karan,
Paco Rabanne, and Thierry Mugler. Not a bad bunch to be associated with, and quite a departure from her previous endorsements –
she had earlier appeared in a Pantene shampoo commercial in
England, her music was used by Renault for a car commercial in
Germany, and Mercedes-Benz also used her in Mexico. In the
summer of 2004, Shapplin sang at the Athens Olympic Games, in
front of 14,000 people. "To me, being famous means that some
people like your music, otherwise it's just a game," she told me.

Evidence of glamour as a game can be seen everywhere, all the time.
"Style icons and rock royalty: Patti Hansen and daughters, Theodora
and Alexandra Richards," reads the caption in an ad for Guerlain's
Shalimar Light, a new scent targeted at the young and trendy, or at least

those who know the three women in the ad as the family of Rolling Stones guitarist Keith Richards. That same ad featured a perfume bottle in the middle ground, wedged between a Fender Telecaster electric guitar (a nice detail, since it's the kind Richards actually plays) and a turntable with a vinyl record already on it ("Introducing Shalimar Light – a new generation rocks a classic," was the only visible copy, as if snappy phraseology were even necessary). The fact that the Richards and Hansen reared their beautiful daughters in suburban Connecticut only added to the legend, of course. There are actually a lot of music people like them, who prefer the social ideal of a small, quiet dinner when they're outside the limelight. Celebrities are normal people, after all; being famous just happens to be their job.

Interestingly, it was the Rolling Stones who first captivated mainstream imagination by going to bed with the advertising world. The perfume company Jovan underwrote the band's 1981 American tour for their album *Tattoo You*. The fashion world itself had always naturally co-opted the flamboyant world of rock, starting with cutting-edge designers like Betsy Johnson and Vivienne Westwood. The American casual clothier Tommy Hilfiger made his mark in the early 1990s by sponsoring the American solo tour of The Who's Pete Townshend. (And his younger brother, Andy Hilfiger, later became Jennifer Lopez's business partner in her company, Sweetface Fashion.)

The late Gianni Versace, of course, gave the world his "frock and roll" aesthetic; everyone was drawn towards making their own nifty variations of the classic credo, "Live fast, die young, and leave a good-looking corpse" (uttered often by Alice Cooper but actually first used in the 1949 film *Knock On Any Door*, said to Humphrey Bogart by John Derek). Particular designers have been mentioned by their celebrity fans, however strange or gauche. Macy Gray announced in July 2004 that she would perform naked to raise money for charity, a once-only show in London for the Elton John AIDS foundation, clad only in her Jimmy Choo heels. Diana Krall wore hers on the cover of her hit album *The Look of Love* and once admonished journalists quick to cite her as just another pretty glamour-chick singer with this admirably sardonic rebuke: "You weren't wearing four-inch Jimmy Choo shoes!"

But it's not really about the shoes.

Glamour, lest anyone should ever forget, is always about the attitude. And the packaging, whether it's a sleek pair of designer pumps or the slickest surfaces conjured by expensive name brands. The best, savviest, and most worldly-wise of celebrities all know this. Nicole Kidman showed up at the world premiere of the film *Mission: Impossible 2* dressed in a sexy, gold-embroidered halter top designed by Michelle Jank – "a 14-karat shimmer," as *Vogue* described the effect in its "Talking Fashion" page, even as many people were prompted to ponder, "Michelle who?" (Jank is an Australian designer, and Kidman was plugging her homeland's creative talents.) Charlize Theron displayed a similar effect on the red carpet at Cannes, decked out in Vera Wang. The idea is deceptively simple – all that glitters is not always gold, but one should always look like a star.

The style matrix

We live in a day and age when an eternal ingénue like Sarah Jessica Parker, star of *Sex and the City*, can win "fashion icon" awards; even the British magazine *New Woman* named Parker as its "Style icon of the year" in 2003. "SJP is the most stylish woman in the world," it gushed in its January 2004 issue. "Not only has she rocked and ruled the fashion roost this year (headscarf, anyone? Leggings?), but we love her for making UK high streets NY hip (she wears it, they copy it, we buy it instantly)." Her onscreen ally Kim Cattrall was awarded "Best taste in mag covers," with a photo of her draped in Armani at the Emmy awards, with SJP alongside her resplendent in Chanel couture. Parker received a Fashion Icon award at the 2004 CDFA (Council of Fashion Designers of America) Fashion awards, held in June 2004, as reported by the Associated Press.

And who can forget Keanu Reeves (with his black trenchcoat, guns stitched into the lining) and Carrie-Ann Moss (with her glistening, black-vinyl catsuit), in the 1999 film *The Matrix* – recalling the futuristic runway fashions of early-1980s Claude Montana and Thierry Mugler. "Whatever the components of style are – confidence, cool, grace, and don't forget black leather – *The Matrix* has it in abundance," wrote science fiction writer Karen Haber in *Exploring the Matrix: Visions of the cyber present*, a collection of essays published in March 2004 that examined the cultural influences of the film. Ruth La Ferla, in the *New York Times* Fashion and Style section, noted how that year's Sean Jean fall collection mirrored Laurence Fishburne's storm coats, and how Christian Dior's quilt-stitched overcoats by Hedi Slimane "all seem to owe a debt to the movie."

Call that life imitating art, especially since certain designers have become stars themselves. Sean Jean, of course, is the fashion line of none other than rap mogul Sean "Puffy" Combs (aka P. Diddy, to those who care), and Kimora Lee Simmons (wife of that other rap mogul, Russell Simmons) is newly famous for her Baby Phat fashions (brought to light to many in the summer of 2004, when she made the news as police patrolmen in New Jersey caught up with her for driving while drugged and then evading arrest; she was "charged with possessing marijuana and avoiding police," reported Jonathan Wald on CNN, on July 29, 2004). The real Cinderella story bar none, however, was the rise and rise of Kate Spade, the former *Mademoiselle* magazine editor who started out selling her designs of nylon tote bags to Barneys and Bergdorf Goodman in New York and now runs a US$70 million company selling handbags, purses, eyeglasses, perfume, and stationery.

In 1999, Spade sold 56 percent of her company to Neiman Marcus for US$33.6 million and entered into a partnership with Estée Lauder. In 2004 her clothing designs debuted, in the form of flight-attendant uniforms for the American budget airline Song. Her company published three lifestyle books – entitled *Manners, Occasions,* and *Style* – to herald the launch of her home collection. Verily, from bags to bedsheets – who needs Martha Stewart, regardless of jail time and Omnimedia stock?

Spade's place in the fashion pantheon was best summarized in *Time* magazine's Spring 2004 "Style and Design" issue, with its cover story: "Women in fashion: who's got the power?" Spade was succinctly described as "the handbag designer who persuaded women in the 90's to trade what she calls 'the nothing black bag' for a purse with personality." It cited her ability to somehow impose her American Midwestern sense of quiet resolve onto women who can be sold the idea of "personality," even where accessories are concerned.

Of course, whether a mere purse can have "personality" depends on the person carrying it. The same *raison d'être* informed the ethos of Miuccia Prada, once a mime student from Milan who turned her family's luggage company into a luxury conglomerate (having achieved, by 2002, US$1.9 billion in revenues). And it all began with a simple black nylon backpack.

However, to the right influential people of the 1990s, that backpack had personality – and Prada goods began carrying an appropriate designer price. Movie stars like Uma Thurman began to be seen in Prada evening gowns at the Oscars. The enigmatic woman herself ("Mrs Prada," as her Italian staff all call her) added to the legend by remaining aloof and mysterious – she still lives in the apartment she grew up in and has very few celebrity friends – but her brand remains one of the best-known in the world, "inspiring" near-perfect knockoffs in all those bootlegging back streets from Bangkok to Beijing. Imitation should be the sincerest form of flattery, in a world where it gets progressively harder to delineate real brand differentiation (especially in the age of mergers, now that Ungaro is part of Ferragamo, Nina Ricci is part of Puig, and then there's a certain French luxury conglomerate called LVMH which married Moët Hennessy with Louis Vuitton).

Not surprisingly, public interest in the celebrity branding arena has grown, to the point where television can sport the likes of *America's Top Model*, the reality television show created and hosted by supermodel Tyra Banks. Celebrity lifestyle magazines became eager to fill their pages with people who evoke glamour, no matter how offbeat (I once asked adult film star Alyssa Klass how she happened to appear in *In Style* magazine, posing in a shimmery-blue Mark Wong Nark gown, and she said she hadn't a clue; "Some guy just took my picture at a party, and the next thing I knew I was in the magazine!") The insatiable need for seeing beautiful people in beautiful clothes had certainly reached epidemic proportions.

Celebrities, of course, enhance the reputation of designers. Christina Ricci appeared in Louis Vuitton's 2004 autumn-winter ads, alongside Hayden Christensen, Chloë Sevigny, Scarlett Johansson, and Helen of Troy herself, the German newcomer Diane Kruger. (Prada's choice for the same season was even edgier, with Maggie Gyllenhaal and Jamie Bell appearing in ads for its Miu Miu label.) The idea itself isn't new; the casual-clothing retailer Gap had made itself famous via its ads featuring celebrities. (Music icons like Willie Nelson, Kris Kristofferson, Marianne Faithfull, Natalie Imbruglia, Taryn Manning; actresses like Sissy Spacek, Isabelle Huppert, and Marlee Matlin – all eclectic, edgy reflections of hip and cool.)

In all these cases, instant brand recognition occurs, because most consumers can instantly recognize those people. (Or if they don't, the ads imply, they should.)

Why, even designer Tom Ford, famous for revamping Gucci into the sexy-attitude luxury label of the 1990s, got into the game. Having left Gucci in the spring of 2004 in an apparent dispute over "creative direction," he launched a book in the autumn of 2004 about his decade at Gucci, with a foreword by *Vogue* editor-in-chief Anna Wintour and pointedly entitled, *Tom Ford*. Nobody will ever mistake him for a maker of automobiles. For he had become his own brand.

In the fickle, flighty world of fashion, Ford had chosen to make his mark in the same way that the late, celebrated photographer Helmut Newton did. By publishing a book, he was announcing to the world his own arrival. In his 2002 autobiography (entitled *Autobiography*), Newton recollected his thoughts about the singular event of 1976 – "the publishing of my first book, *White Women*. It was very important at this stage in my career, because a book gives a photographer an authority that magazines and newspapers can never offer . . . The book made a furor because it was the first of its kind. The term 'porno chic' was coined in connection with it."

Newton's sexually-charged photos of women in various stages of undress, always posed in exotic locations, paved the way for what some 30 years later we merely take for granted. In the book, he also made specific mention of how he favored editorial work over advertising, simply because editorial work meant his name would be credited. He wanted to "become a famous photographer," and he realized "Helmut Newton" was a brand name, one that needed repeated exposure to the world for him to achieve his goal. Outrage and shock could only conspire to help him, and so they did.

Newton's success underscored one of the more obvious facets of modern celebrity – the constant surveillance of the media, a by-product of the envy they provoke. Consider, for example, the case of supermodel Naomi Campbell, who told the *Guardian* in London of her hectic schedule for just one week in June 2004. She hadn't stayed in any one place for 48 hours: "I was in Brazil, in Sao Paulo, then here for one night. Athens, here for two nights. Then to Paris, Paris to Hamburg, Milan in one day, then Milan to Brazil, Brazil to New York for one day, back to Brazil, Brazil to here for one day, then back to Brazil." To be alone in an airplane, she disclosed, was "very quiet and very calming . . . Sometimes, I'm not on a plane for 10 days, and I get like, aaargh, I need to get on a plane." Agence France-Presse, the French wire service, picked up the piece and circulated it, lending further mystique to the celebrityhood of Naomi Campbell.

Previously, in 1994, Campbell had decided to spread her wings and record an album (*Babywoman*, released on Sony Music's Epic label) and even pen a novel. The book, *Swan*, a *roman à clef* about the fashion world, was actually ghostwritten by one Caroline Upcher; Campbell, for lending her name to the project, received an advance of US$200,000. "Naomi was instrumental in developing the plot and the characters," Campbell's publicist told reporter Erica Kornberg of *Entertainment Weekly*. "Plenty of books have ghostwriters." *Swan*, of course, pre-dated Pamela Anderson's novel *Star* by a decade.

How could anyone not find amusing such cultural subterfuge? In truth, many celebrities partner with writers, usually celebrity jour-nalists, to "co-write" books. The writer interviews the celebrity, tran-scribes hours of tape, and then reworks the celebrity's words into an acceptable, written form. The projects are assembled by the writers' literary agents, pitched and sold to publishing houses, and remuner-ation is negotiated with every eye on the contract – the bigger the celebrity, the smaller the amount the co-writer usually gets. A 70/30 split is often the best a celebrity journalist can expect, excellent given that that sometimes the paltry 30 percent doesn't even exist at all – some celebrities will insist on the writer receiving merely a flat fee.

Celebrity branding thrives on such dogged determination and meticulous effort, in a ready market in which the real commodity is hero-worship. It feeds on the need that so many people have for validation, even if we now live in a time of decentralized pop iconography. Marketers are fighting even harder for their piece of the pie, and what has evidently transpired is that more and more celebrities are manufactured to gird this incessant fray. A greater array, and more choices, such have become the benchmarks of our postmodern civilization. Fashion, arguably more than any other field of creative endeavor, depends on such plenitude.

There is then, an overarching idea – one of possession, much like the way oil paintings in the days of Renaissance Europe were the precursors of consumer frenzy. We are what we possess, hence their ascribed value. As art historians have persuasively argued, the Cubist painters then took this one step further. Georges Braque and Pablo Picasso founded the movement by incorporating everyday objects into their paintings and collages – "Still Life on a Table," with its ads for Gillette razors excised from a newspaper, remains a Braque masterpiece. And then, in the modern age, along came Andy Warhol with his three-dimensional Brillo box sculptures and his Campbell's soup cans. Such were the first big statements in art about branding. The man who now buys Ermenegildo Zegna suits and then feels validated when the actor Adrien Brody appears in the designer's print ads is, metaphorically, the same man who buys a Warhol from an art dealer – because of the delicate brushing of auras that occurs, when a famous person has laid his mark on something, akin to the way farmers branded cattle as signs of ownership.

Ownership is the prize, even in this evanescent field called fashion. We read about designers all the time, but always pay heed when their celebrity customers are mentioned. For instance, Vivienne Tam, the New York-based designer whose work reflects her own Hong Kong-Chinese roots, is now worn by Julia Roberts, Britney Spears, and Madonna.

Roberts's dress, bought for her by her then-beau Benjamin Bratt, was the very one featuring Tam's most famous design: her print of Kuan Yin, the Chinese goddess of mercy, which now hangs in the permanent archives of the Museum of the Fashion Institute of Technology, in New York. That it would be housed in a museum is poetic and poignant, since it serves to remind us that we do need our goddesses. To remind us, naturally, of who we are.

Kim-Van Dang

Kim-Van Dang is Beauty Director at the celebrity magazine *In Style*, in New York, where she oversees its editorial coverage of beauty products. The Saigon-born, Vietnamese-American previously worked at *Women's Wear Daily* in Los Angeles, where she wrote about her shopping trips with supermodels Amber Valletta and Kate Moss, though nothing compares with the night she met her movie idol, the Armani-clad Jeremy Irons, while covering the Oscars.

Do you have a favorite funny or interesting anecdote about dealing with a celebrity?

They're all rather nice to me. They have their fair share of hair-disaster stories, skincare issues, and make-up obsessions. Just like the rest of us.

What do you think has been In Style *magazine's biggest contribution to public awareness of celebrities in terms of fashion/lifestyle?*

In Style was the first magazine to show a celebrity on the red carpet from head to toe, so that readers could see that aside from the gown, what handbag, what shoes and even what toe polish color she is wearing. It seems simple, but that concept didn't exist until we created it. And the style in *In Style* goes beyond the outfits. It's really the first celebrity lifestyle magazine, where readers get to learn not just what's in a star's closet, but what kind of face cream she favors, why she dyed her hair or cut it short and how she feels about the change, what her home is like, who her gal pals are, whether she loves dogs or cats, what her favorite dish to cook is, where she got that great lamp and which philanthropic causes she cares deeply about. *In Style* shows celebrities not simply as beautiful, rich, and famous, but as real people that real people can relate to. This was a breakthrough concept when the magazine launched ten years ago.

Do you think people read In Style *more for the celebrity coverage or for the fashion/glamour coverage?*

I like to say that *In Style* is a how-to service book disguised as a glam, glossy one. There's no question that our readers love celebrities, but they also love the magazine because of all the information jam-packed in it.

What is your general feeling about famous people and "brand extension"? Do you think someone like Christy Turlington is more justified in doing her yoga clothing line than say Jennifer Lopez with her perfumes?

I don't think celebrities need to justify what they endorse. It's their business. They choose their affiliations wisely and use the top stylists and photographers in these campaigns. I can't think of an instance when their celebrity image has been compromised.

But do you think that women today pay too much attention to celebrities and they way they dress and live, because they are conditioned to become dependent on them as paragons of style?

In the end, a woman likes what she likes: silhouettes that look good on her body type, colors that compliment her hair, eye and skin tones, style that expresses her personality and work for her lifestyle. She might idolize a certain celebrity but she will wear what makes her comfortable, be it a pair of flats or stilettos.

Do you think that celebrities are normal people who dress better? Or do they know how to dress because they have more money to indulge in style?

Some celebrities have great taste. Others have great stylists.

5
Edifice Rex: Celebrity and Brand Extension

In December 2003, Eric Clapton acquired a 50 percent stake in the English clothing company Cordings of Piccadilly and was said to be "supervising its relaunch as the home of traditional country clothing." This did not surprise anyone, since Clapton's fame had previously been extended by an array of other merchandising elements.

Through deals with the clothing company Stussy in Los Angeles and the celebrity merchandising company Fan Asylum in San Francisco, Clapton already had an array of items for sale, both on his official website and at his concerts. All these carried his famous "EC" signature logo – emblazoned on T-shirts, sweatshirts, jackets, windbreakers, coffee mugs, keychains, and baseball caps.

His being the co-owner of a "traditional country clothing" maker, however, made perfect sense. Books about the Clapton legend pointed to facts that implied a very congruent branding situation; Clapton still lived in Ripley, the little Surrey hamlet where he was born, and his spare time was often spent out in the woods, focussing on a hobby highly peculiar for a rock star – fishing.

This made for a suitably admirable mythology, which could be traded in commercial terms. Marketers call this "brand extension" – similar to what happens when a cigarette company like Marlboro gets into the business of producing and selling outdoor clothing, yet different in the sense that a famous person and not a corporate entity was now the product being marketed.

People buy Eric Clapton or Marlboro clothing depending on the mental and emotional associations they foster about Eric Clapton or Marlboro. The same applies to, say, Dunhill and its departure from being a cigarette maker to a maker of finely crafted luxury goods (watches, pens, attaché cases, and the like). In some cases, though, this kind of thing works too well and crosses a fine line between the real and the surreal.

One such case occurred in 2003, when the Clos du Bois winery of Sonoma County, California, unveiled a new wine brand in honour of the late Jerry Garcia, the frontman of the rock band the Grateful Dead. Called J. Garcia wines (in line with his more famous and already available J. Garcia neckties), the first shipment of 22,000 cases sold out in just 30 days, prompting a second batch – comprising 30,000 cases of Cabernet Sauvignon, Zinfandel, and Merlot – to be issued in early 2004.

What was interesting about this? The fact that Jerry Garcia himself was not a wine connoisseur, let alone much of a wine drinker. "Quite honestly, Jerry was not really a big drinker," admitted Dennis McNally, the long-time publicist and biographer of the Grateful Dead, in a June 13, 2004 Associated Press interview. Garcia's abstract paintings, however, did appear on the wine labels. This was done with the permission of the Garcia estate.

Clearly, somebody came up with the brilliant idea to exploit his artistic talent. Garcia had attended the San Francisco Art Institute, and in his youth was often divided between art and music. So what if he didn't drink wine much?

Given the rapid blitz of those first 22,000 cases – an exceptionally good sales result in the wine business – there were clearly enough people enamoured of Garcia's name to partake of the vintage. This, of course, was done to also boost the branding of Clos du Bois (reputedly a fairly good, though not exceptional, wine maker), However, it wasn't as if Garcia was a complete teetotaler. As Dennis McNally conceded, "He did have his occasional glass of wine." Like Eric Clapton and his clothing lines, this was not an entirely bogus enterprise. It could even be viewed as clever, and a celebration of (so to speak) the spirit.

This differs from cases where the celebrity doesn't use or endorse the product at all, and others have wholly profited from the enterprise. The best case in point might well be the strange phenomenon of Madonna condoms.

Madonna box sets

"Can I have an exotic, ribbed, strawberry Madonna, please?" might sound weird, but in countries like Malaysia and Singapore where they're openly sold in pharmacies and supermarkets, such a request can be commonplace indeed. Madonna condoms come in boxes of three (priced at about US$2 a box), and each box features an image of Madonna – culled from a set shot in 1979 by photographer Martin Schreiber. Madonna was then a nude model for a photography class that Schreiber was teaching, "Photographing the nude," at an art school in New York.

She was not at all a star then (and would not be for another five years), and came in to Schreiber's studio and posed for him – with no inkling of how this would later become historic, for reasons she would dread to recall.

Fatefully, she signed release forms authorizing Schreiber's owner-ship of all the photos he took without limitation of time, country, or usage. Madonna was over 18 at the time, and her signature gave Schreiber the rights to international use of the photos. It was this that she came to regret later, when she unsuccessfully contested his right to use them for other purposes.

In 2001, Schreiber sold those photos to a company called VDM International in the Netherlands, which then sold the American rights to a sex toy and condom company called Condomania. But he had apparently decided to exploit his association with Madonna even before the sale to VDM. In 1990, he published the photos under the title *Madonna Nudes 1979* in Germany, and then signed a deal, involving a "license and sales agreement on copyrights" regarding those photos, with one Francis Bernard Clement.

He basically licensed the worldwide rights to Clement, who then appointed sub-licensees to manufacture, distribute, promote, and sell the images on products worldwide. One of these sub-licensees, a Malaysian company called NR Synergy, undertook the task of manufacturing, distributing, promoting, and selling them in South-east Asia in 1999. And that's how Madonna condoms, which come in six colours as well as in "exotic ribbed," "contoured," and "strawberry" flavors, ended up on the racks in Malaysia and Singapore.

The photos on the condom boxes were cropped from Schreiber's black-and-white portraits, all featuring Madonna in her natural brunette tresses and pouting one step short of a frown; rather apro-pos, since she reportedly remained upset about the use of these images but had no legal recourse.

The example of Madonna is interesting because it demonstrates how certain images of certain celebrities have a shelf-life that neither of the participants could originally have imagined. The reason Schreiber's enterprising efforts paid off simply rested on the fact that Madonna, at the time he sealed the deal with Clement, had become an international superstar. (1990 was the year of her stylish, controversial drag queen-influenced "Vogue" video and her acclaimed *Blonde Ambition* tour). The inherent value of her image was obvious, and consumers used to making the mental association (instantly linking Madonna with sex, of course) would inevitably be drawn to purchase these condoms.

The example of Madonna condoms is merely a more perverse way of how successful "brand extension" works. As marketing expert Wally Olins noted in his book *On Brand*, "it says that a particular brand has a life and personality of its own. If the emotions surrounding it are sufficiently powerful, we will unquestioningly accept its functional capabilities."

In the world of household goods (and more mundane material items), Olins noticed major companies had been "shifting their ground" from making and selling to being. This, of course, seems more than sensible in the entertainment world, since celebrities need only be in order to sell, and what they are usually selling are expressions of themselves.

This applies even when others do the selling, for reasons less avaricious than condoms. The late Johnny Cash's personal items were auctioned at Sotheby's in New York (his guitars, black leather boots, seven Grammy awards, his 1987 Rolls Royce, and even a tin cup that he once received from a warden at Folsom Prison during his famous 1968 performance; the tin cup was valued at US$600!).

Eric Clapton, of course, auctioned off many of his own guitars to benefit his Crossroads Centre, a halfway house for recovering drug addicts; Some sold for US$150,000 and one particular favorite of his for US$450,000. Clean and sober after years of battling addiction himself, he was now taking the opportunity to pay back. "I had everything I could want," Clapton said in the opening mission statement on the concert DVD (*Eric Clapton and Friends in Concert: A benefit for the Crossroads Centre at Antigua*). "I was a millionaire, I had beautiful women in my life and a solid-gold career. And a future. And yet on a daily basis, I wanted to commit suicide." Who could fail to be swayed by such a heartfelt plea?

Lifestyle product extensions

And now for something completely different: The ever-beautiful Jennifer Lopez and her ever-burgeoning fragrance line.

"In the eye of the storm, I am ... Still," read the ad copy for her scent called Still; more rapturous verses follow on her beauty products website and online store. Lopez called her business venture Sweetface Fashion, a partnership between her and Andy Hilfiger (the younger brother of designer Tommy Hilfiger) which began in April 2001. The idea, her company bio posited, was "to develop a fashion collection under her creative direction ... to reflect her personal style by being sexy, fun and fashionable."

The venture started off by launching a junior sportswear collection (called JLO by Jennifer Lopez) and then ventured into "lifestyle product extensions" – her first perfume Glow, and then swimwear (JLO Swim) and a separate license with the company Outlook Eyewear for JLO Sunglasses.

Glow, her website emphasized, is a perfume for "capturing angelic, glistening sensuality." Lopez even explained it herself, in an interview segment on the site: "It represents everything I've loved ever since I was very young – fresh, clean, simple, sensual things. Things like fresh air, the breeze coming in through the window, the ocean, summer sunshine. People might have expected a Jennifer Lopez fragrance to be more musky, more overtly sexy, but Glow by JLO is much more the real me, rather than the two-dimensional image you seen on screen or in a magazine."

The lush, shimmery photos of her on the site don't much reflect her Bronx roots and she appeared to have come a long, long way from the housing projects of Castle Hill where she grew up. "I never say I'm from New York, I always say I'm from the Bronx, because that's where I'm from," she told me, when I met her in January 2001.

Her merchandising company hadn't started up yet. "And I guess, in a way, it is rags to riches. I'm that same girl who grew up in the Bronx and who wanted to act and wanted to sing and wanted to dance, and I worked really hard to try to make that happen.

"I've always focused on wanting to be good. I wanted to be the best that I could be. As an artist, I always wanted to grow and to sing, and to continue growing as an actress. That's always what's driven me. To get the next better part. To get better in that role. To be good in it. You know what I mean?"

Getting the next part, initially, meant leveraging on her new-found fame after she'd played the lead in *Selena*, the true story of the slain Mexican-American singer Selena Quintanilla, and then became the highest-paid Latina actress (earning US$1 million a movie); the next step was recording her debut album in 1999. She entitled it *On the 6* – named after the subway train she used to take into Manhattan from the Bronx for her dance rehearsals. As cryptic as the title was, word spread about her desire to succeed, as embodied by that number 6 train, enough to help her score a hit album. Such are the things we love about pop culture, the creation of urban legend and lore.

The success of Jennifer Lopez as a pop star came at the tail end of a decade when record companies began to get clever about packaging items in "co-branded" ways, so as to stand out amid the clutter. Warner Bros. Records was one of the first to attempt to exploiting this when it released *Dream*, the debut album of actress Tia Carrere in 1993.

The exotic Eurasian beauty, fresh off her sizzling role in the 1992 hit movie *Wayne's World*, should have seen it as a premature move; her visibility then was still too limited for mainstream success, and the album sank without a trace. Other actresses followed suit, a revolving door of multifaceted talents from Milla Jovovich (with her album *The Divine Comedy* in 1994) to Jennifer Love Hewitt (with her album *BareNaked* in 2002), with equally underwhelming results. Most people just couldn't buy the idea that an actress could also sing. The days of Judy Garland and Liza Minnelli seemed over, almost as if the modern marketplace at large could not handle anyone with such a surfeit of talent. Singers trying to act, of course, usually fared worse (Madonna being the prime contender, and some would say Faith Hill was a good choice as merely one of *The Stepford Wives*).

The perfect scam

Sometimes, however, only selected target markets are made privy to such branding. David Hasselhoff, the *Baywatch* star, has had hit albums only in Germany. Japan always comes to mind – scores of actors and actresses have recorded albums that have never been released in their home countries. Alyssa Milano, the nymphette star of the television series *Charmed*, for instance, has had five albums released but only in Japan. All of them have sold and "gone platinum" (in Japan, that's 200,000 copies of each), and all because of a sequence of events triggered by public demand.

The film *Commando*, in which she'd starred with Arnold Schwarzenegger, was shown in Japan when she was 15 years old. "It was the first time Japan had seen me," she told *FHM* magazine (the American edition's January/February 2001 issue), "and the fans started writing in to magazines asking, 'Who is this girl?' So I did some interviews over there and said I'd been in (the musical) *Annie*. A record company exec saw that, assumed I could sing, and gave me a five-album contract! It was so bizarre, I had to do it."

Prior to *Commando*, Milano had spent eight years on the television sitcom *Who's the Boss?* so stardom did not faze her. She had starred in the *Melrose Place* series before *Charmed* (as the kid sister of Shannen Doherty and Holly Marie Combs), and then acquired further attention for running a website specializing in the image protection of celebrities. She'd apparently seen too many nude photos of herself used without her permission.

"I'm not ashamed of the nudity I've done," she noted (in the same interview). "It wasn't about that. It's about the porn masters making US$30,000 a month off my naked body without my permission. We had twelve lawsuits, all of which were settled outside of court. We did go to trial for one case and we won a quarter of a million dollars."

(*E! Online* on September 19, 1999 reported that "Milano won a judgement for US$238,000 against a Minnesota man who illegally posted her photos.")

Milano's forthrightness recalls an issue pertinent to any discussion of celebrity: Sometimes, celebrity images are used to sell records even when the celebrity has either very superficial or peripheral, or worse still, no bearing at all on the music. Some don't perform at all on them, and the companies issuing them presume that enough fools and their money will be easily parted.

An excellent example was Jenny McCarthy's *Surfin' Safari*, a 1996 compilation of surf music classics (from Jan and Dean to the Beach Boys to the Ventures) fronted by the lovely Miss McCarthy, then riding high as an MTV host and the 1994 *Playboy* "Playmate of the Year," who appeared on the CD artwork – on the cover, the inside sleeve, the back cover, the disc itself (only her bikini-bottomed derrière), and, lest anyone forget, even on an autographed fold-out poster that came with the CD.

At the time of release, McCarthy was the host of MTV's *Singled Out* – a dating show and one of the precursors of today's reality television craze – and she had some very savvy instincts about her personal branding. When writer Douglas Tseng, then an *MTV Asia* writer/producer, asked her about being a sex symbol (in *BigO* magazine, January 1997), she replied: "Even in the past, people used it as a commodity, and they still do. People will still buy pin-ups, no matter what generation it is. People like sex and there's no way around it. It's a matter of how you want to show it to the world.

"Marilyn Monroe did it her way, which was the voluptuous sex-goddess. Pamela Anderson was the *Baywatch* bathing suit babe, that was her kinda way. Mine is kinda more ... to look into the mirror and making fun of myself instead of taking it so seriously." At that time, her autobiography, *Jen-X: Jenny McCarthy's open book*, had not been published. The fact that it eventually came out and bombed might have been a factor for her fast fade from the limelight.

Her "surf album" bombed too, probably because not enough people wanted to buy into her self-deprecating ideology. Girls in bikinis look good next to surfboards; they don't look good picking their nose (as she was seen doing in *Rolling Stone*). McCarthy exhibited unusual courage in satirizing her own iconography, a rare thing for a glamour model, but it damaged her branding. This was compounded by the inescapable fact that McCarthy wasn't a musician herself and even her "surfer girl" persona was entirely manufactured, since she hailed from the South Side of Chicago, with nary a beach in sight. The credibility gap had been over-strained, to her detriment.

An object lesson in brand extension, however, was the CD *Jackie Collins Presents Lethal Seduction*, which went places Jenny McCarthy never did. Released in July 2000, it was deftly packaged as a "companion" to the novel of the same name, featuring songs that were chosen because, as the album's press release put it, they involved "themes that are addressed throughout her novels."

This closed the credibility gap nicely, since sex and seduction have been characters themselves in the Jackie Collins literary canon. The songs on the CD all dealt with seduction, as sung by the likes of Aretha Franklin, Dionne Warwick, Ike and Tina Turner, Blondie, Dusty Springfield, Eartha Kitt, Sister Sledge, and the ever-so-catchy All Saints song from 1998, "Lady Marmalade" (with its charming, hypnotic "Voulez vous coucher avec moi, ce soir?" chorus). Collins, the publicity bio added, also made her recording debut on the title track as its "sexy ambient narrator."

To whet the appetite, she even penned a personal note in the CD booklet, repeated in the official press bio that went out to reviewers: "Songs have the ability to trigger powerful memories, and favorite songs seem to create our own life's soundtrack. The songs included here have taken me back in time and around the world, and the result is an exciting party CD, as well as the perfect accompaniment to an afternoon by the pool."

The bio carried the headline, "Power, Sex, Hollywood & Jackie Collins!" while her own note in the CD had the headline: "Sex! Passion! Danger! Romance!" and ended with a facsimile of her autograph.

Collins, by lending her name to this project in her personal voice, gave it a tremendous "value-added" cachet, and the art direction added a touch of class: the CD booklet featured a holographic cover that mirrored the cover of the book, complete with the words "Lethal Seduction" in the style of lipstick on a mirror. The idea was to evoke ambience, so that one can partake of "a compilation of dramatic songs that confront matters of the heart," as the press bio described it.

How this is done, of course, is a routine matter at most record companies today: The label's "strategic marketing" department, which assembles and markets all compilation albums (such as film soundtracks and "greatest hits" collections), will make an arrangement with the book's publisher (Simon & Schuster, in Collins's case), although sometimes the deal will be negotiated by the author's own literary agent (especially if the author is a famous name). The terms depend on the star-power of both author and agent, working on the theory that it will be a win–win, "co-branding" victory for both parties.

Rhino Records, in this particular case, expedited the Jackie Collins project through its ancillary arm, Rhino Entertainment Ventures, though the album itself was created by a three-man production team (Bruce Roberts, Dave Munk, and Greg Mertz, but under the auspices of an entity called Chalkboard Music, headed by Collins herself as "executive producer"). Quite an endeavor it must have been, especially since such compilations typically involve clearing multiple copyrights, for many songs by different artists (14 of them, on *Jackie Collins Presents Lethal Seduction*). What's interesting, of course, is the clash of celebrity auras, given the fact that so many artists get heard in the context of a single theme.

Personal passions

The same thing applies when artists get their music used in commercials, leading some to lampoon this idea. The folk/pop singer Jewel did so in her famous "Intuition" video, in the summer of 2003, which featured numerous brand names and logos, obviously a self-deprecating parody since she herself had signed an endorsement deal with Schick, for a new feminine razor called "Intuition" – with the tag line "Trust your intuition" (of course).

Jewel might have been inspired by the potential for parody that had long existed in the rap world, ever since the group Run-DMC recorded their song "My Adidas" as a tribute to the famous athletic shoe. The cynics who scoffed at African-American youths and their fetish for sneakers weren't laughing, though, when Run-DMC then secured an endorsement contract with the shoe company itself.

That trailblazing deal was the brainchild of the group's manager Russell Simmons, co-founder of Def Jam Records. "Russell Simmons and his Rush Management team were determined to turn that record's message into money," observed the black music archivist Nelson George, in his 1998 book *Hip Hop America*. In 1986, Simmons arranged for Run-DMC to play a concert at Madison Square Garden in New York, with several Adidas executives from Germany in the audience. During the song "My Adidas," the group asked audience members to hold up their Adidas sneakers, and the executives were enthralled to witness a sea of three-striped shoes hovering in the air.

Backstage after the show, the group was told by the German team that they could have their own Adidas clothing line. Rush Management closed a deal with Adidas for US$1.5 million, whereby the rappers would get to show off their own Run DMC sneakers, jerseys, and other accessories. Following this, other rappers obtained similar deals (Whodini with Lacoste Sportif, L.L. Cool J with Troop). Simmons went on create the garment enterprise Phat Farm ("classic American flava with a twist"), now a US$263 million company that includes a sports line called Run Athletics. He also served as an adviser to Motorola and Courvoisier, on "how to sell to the urban market," as an October 2003 *Business Week* feature on him noted.

The field is still wide open for new deals, given the endurance of the genre. Eminem, the premier rapper of our time, has already sold almost 20 million copies worldwide of his 2002 album *The Eminem Show*; in late 2004, he launched his own hip-hop channel with Sirius Satellite Radio, on which he introduced acts from his own Shady Records imprint. The field remains his for the taking.

The strangest music-related deal of all, however, might be the one in which the English singer/songwriter Nick Drake achieved posthumous success, when his song "Pink Moon" was used in a Volkswagen commercial in the United States in 2000, a whole 25 years after his death. Well, why not have celebrities sell cars? Or lingerie, since even Bob Dylan has now been in a Victoria's Secret commercial?

In 1995 the esteemed rock critic Greil Marcus, the most astute of Dylan observers, wrote that it did not bother him that Dylan had licensed his 1960s protest song "The Times They Are A-Changin'" to be used in a television commercial for the Coopers & Lybrand accounting firm. "I think all songs should go up on this block," Marcus wrote in *Interview* magazine. "It's a way of finding out if songs that carry people with them, songs that seem tied to a particular time and place, can survive a radical recontextualization, or if that recontextualization dissolves them."

Dylan allowed the same song to be used again in 1996, in a commercial for the Bank of Montreal, as if he still wasn't sure if the recontextualization had taken hold. But Marcus had a point. Celebrity is in the eyes and ears of the beholder, and it is an intriguing aspect of any mainstream artistic endeavour to test the parameters of accessibility.

If a demi-god falls in the forest, will his acolytes hear if he makes no sound? And perhaps that's why no one should be surprised to read of how the fashion designer Stella McCartney, daughter of the famous Beatle Paul, brand-extended herself following her successful tenures at Chloé and Gucci, to ink a deal with Adidas for the "Adidas by Stella McCartney sport performance collection," launched in February 2005 in the United States, Japan, and Europe.

Or that Maria Sharapova, the fetching Russian lass who won the 2004 Wimbledon ladies tennis trophy signed a three-year, US$5 million contract with the perfume company Parlux to launch a scent carrying her name at the end of 2004. Sharapova had earlier signed a US$4 million deal with Motorola, her first endorsement following her Wimbledon victory. (Some claim this to be a mobile phone joke, but the deal actually happened.)

Bill Wasserzieher, the veteran blues music critic for *Blues Revue*, once jokingly remarked to me that his favorite blues musician name wasn't Blind Blake, Blind Lemon Jefferson, or Blind Willie McTell, but "Blind Lemon Pledge." He was referring to the fact that the very name of a celebrity now carries a certain value, undiminished by multiple practical guises. This is what accounts for all those celebrity restaurants – Gloria Estefan (Larios, in Miami); Jennifer Lopez (Madre's, in Pasadena, California); and poor Britney Spears once had Nyla, her Louisiana-themed New York eatery, which she has since disowned.

Robert DeNiro remains one of the founding partners in the highly successful, high-end Japanese restaurant chain Nobu. Johnny Depp co-owns the Viper Room nightclub in Los Angeles and the Man Ray restaurant in Paris. Even a cult celebrity like the electronic dance/trance genius Moby owns a Manhattan cafe called Teany, designed with citrus-bright colours and featured in *Elle Décor*, in September 2002. ("The vegetarian menu is heavy on connoisseur-quality teas but light on attitude," charmingly urged the review, which ran with a photo of a beaming, bespectacled Moby sitting *al fresco* on the patio.)

And well, why not? Celebrity endorsements are possibly the best part of being a celebrity, since one's essence is used to enhance a product. Rock singer Joan Jett disclosed in an interview with writer Chauncc Hayden, in *Penthouse* magazine in October 1999, that her biggest regret was not accepting the commercial deals that were offered to her. Jett had made it a personal policy to not accept commercial endorsements for fear of compromising her non-corporate rock image, a decision she later came to regret.

"In the past, I have believed that rock 'n' roll stood for something and that bands shouldn't endorse things," she told Hayden. "I said no to the tune of a million and a half dollars ... (for) putting a car in a video. Just putting a car in a scene, just sitting there on a street. I didn't have to say, 'Buy this' or anything. I mean, a car had to be in the video anyway.... Looking back, I think I was very stupid.

"Because there ain't nobody coming up to me saying, 'Way to go, Joan, for not taking millions of dollars for rock 'n' roll, man. That really meant something!' Nobody has said shit. And I'm out millions of bucks.... I would never make that mistake again.... I was just very stubborn."

She might have read that Isabella Rossellini, at age 30, had earned US$35,000 a year for just 35 days' work posing as the face of Lancôme cosmetics. By the time her contract ended in 1996, had made US$2.79 million from Lancôme alone. All this and the fact that Rossellini, in interviews, has admitted to discomfort with advertising – or rather, as she put it in an interview with Britain's *Observer*, published on July 10, 2004, with "what the world of surfaces stands for."

Well, that depends entirely on the surface, or what it represents Just before he died in 2003, the sardonic singer/songwriter Warren Zevon reminisced, for a VH-1 documentary on his life, about having his friend Bruce Springsteen come into the studio to record with him. "The thing about Springsteen," Zevon observed, "is that he is exactly the person that everybody hopes he would be." His everyman, working-class hero persona is no publicity ploy; Springsteen's fame has rested solidly on his very real, actual countenance. He is edifice as a means of faith and hope.

The same thing happened in September 1997, when Bob Dylan sang his famous song, "Knockin' on Heaven's Door" to none other than the Pope, John Paul II, at an outdoor concert for the World Eucharistic Congress in Bologna, Italy, in front of 200,000 people. The *Los Angeles Times* reported the event as "a brief encounter choreographed in to broaden the Roman Catholic Church's appeal to Italian youth."

The pontiff, then 77, even spoke to the crowd by quoting Dylan – from "Blowin' in the Wind," a song of existentialist questioning, retold the Pope's way: "How many roads must a man walk down, before he becomes a man? I answer you: One. There is only one road for man, and it is Christ." In the end, it might seem, we use our celebrities to suit our needs.

In such light, a hallmark of celebrity is to prove useful as a lifestyle conduit, or a catalyst of change. There may be no greater gift than this gift of a certain romance, implied by a look or an attitude – one etched in memory, because of what we can see and hear and touch, becoming our personal passions forever.

Bill Wasserzieher

Bill Wasserzieher is a veteran music journalist, formerly with the *Village Voice* in New York and best-known as a blues critic with *Blues Revue*. Based in Long Beach, California, he spent seven years working for the Knight-Ridder newspaper chain and has been a publicity writer for numerous record companies.

Who was the most interesting celebrity you've met?

Sylvester Stallone. I did an early interview with him on the set of *F.I.S.T.*, his 1977 film with director Norman Jewison. Sly was astonishingly open about his good fortune at the time and very funny and self-deprecating. He's one of the few actors I've met who actually seemed happy in his life. Of course he hadn't made that error in marital judgment with Brigitte Nielsen at the time.

Do you have any funny stories to share about the process of creating publicity material?

A few years ago, I did liner notes for a reissue of an album by the guitarist Bert Jansch, of Pentangle fame. I'm an ex-academic, so I know how to research, which is what I did. I came up with a lot of interesting material from circa 1969–70, and after I finished the text, I faxed it to the local store on the isolated island where Bert lives, off the coast of Scotland. About a week or so later, when he came in for supplies, he read it. He faxed back that he didn't remember some of the events I described, but he'd take my word on the fact that they happened. To steal from a John Ford film, sometimes you print the legend.

How do you feel about writing publicity bios, in general?

I've written dozens of publicity bios, sometimes with the aid of the subject but more often without. It's usually easier the latter way. Musicians, actors, and writers aren't necessarily interesting people. What publicity does is merge the artist with the art, the person with the product. That's not necessarily a good thing, but that's how marketing works. It puts faces on commodities.

Do you think we will reach a saturation point with regard to celebrity obsession?

We are already beyond the saturation point. Nothing happens without publicity these days. No film gets a major release without the stars making the rounds of talk shows; no major artist's CD goes into the store bins without a full-court press from label publicists; no book goes onto the shelves without the author doing a tour. Modern life, at least in the Western world, revolves around celebrities, even to the point where there are celebrities who are famous for simply being famous.

Do you have a theory for why this has happened?

Western philosophers used to talk about there being a crisis in Christendom, that a centre no longer existed to hold together elements that were spinning off in different directions. Religious issues aside, it's probably true. People today are without an ordered universe. They are at loose ends. With 24-hour media overwhelming us, a simple life lived in obscurity is no longer enough. We've come to want more, expect more, demand more, and to be frustrated by anything less. Just look at celebrity stalkers. They need to add value to their lives by attaching themselves to those who are famous. And it needn't be just actors or musicians. Imprisoned serial killers get plenty of love letters.

What's your opinion of celebrity "co-branding" vis-à-vis product endorsements?

Does Jaclyn Smith, an aging Charlie's Angel, need to attach her name to a cheap clothing line at Kmart? I suppose if it pays the bills and allows her some retention of fame. But it must be a bit embarrassing.

Since you have an interest in aviation yourself, what do you think of John Travolta as a pilot and pitchman?

John Travolta has an arrangement with Qantas whereby he gives them a certain number of days a year for publicity, and the airline pays him handsomely and lets him exercise his love of flying. It's a way of keeping his name out there without having to deliver a successful film. It also helps counteract the Scientology stigma he carries. It's better than having to do actual commercials.

You once taught English at a college in New York, during which time you occupied the very office that used to belong to Philip Roth. What was that like, being in the long shadow of a famous predecessor?

I had trouble writing, especially after I found out that I had been assigned the office where Philip Roth wrote *Portnoy's Complaint*. I felt unworthy to be there until the department secretary, who had typed his manuscript, told me in response to my question about whether she had been offended by the sex scenes: "No, I was just typing words. I didn't actually read them."

6
Epics and Enigmas: The Lure of Asian Exotica

If the incident hadn't occurred, a publicist would've invented it. As legend has it, Michelle Yeoh remembers the day she received a certain visitor in 1996, at the hospital where she was recuperating from a stunt accident. She'd dived off an overpass while filming and missed some cardboard boxes placed to break her fall, crashing onto the pavement below. "My back went snap," she later recalled. Luckily, she had not broken any bones.

Her deep-tissue bruises, however, would take several months to heal. Meantime, the visitor, a fan from Los Angeles, cheered her up immensely. He sat by her bedside and recounted, from memory, all her most daring film stunts – as only the most diehard of fans can do.

His name was Quentin Tarantino.

Later that same year, I was talking with Hong Kong director Ringo Lam about his Hollywood career. His 1987 film *City on Fire* was acknowledged as the inspiration for the film that would launch Quentin Tarantino's own career, *Reservoir Dogs*, and so he was now in the limelight himself. His new big-budget action flick *Maximum Risk*, starring Jean-Claude Van Damme and Natasha Hentsridge, had opened at number one in the US box office. This was proof, surely, that the Hong Kong method of combining clever stunts with stylish camera placement could sell in America.

"Hollywood pictures are recognized worldwide and dominate movie markets everywhere in the world," Lam said to me, "and that tells us something   that audiences are used to the Hollywood film language." But he shared the same grievances as his compatriot John Woo, lamenting the endless meetings and strict union rules that restricted his creative freedom.

"In Hong Kong, the financier just comes to me and says he'll give me so-much money if I'll work with Chow Yun-fat and deliver the movie six months afterwards and make sure it's an action drama. And that's it. That's the Hong Kong way. In Hollywood, the budgets are so big that they can afford to close down entire streets for shooting. In Hong Kong, we have to watch out for the traffic and shoot at the same time!"

"In Hong Kong, everything's much simpler," John Woo had told me, a few months earlier. "One meeting and you can make a movie.

I never knew there were so many problems to making films in Hollywood. A lot of things were so frustrating. Like the politics, the games, the meetings, and everything. It was quite an experience. After my first Hollywood film, *Hard Target*, I stopped making movies for almost two years."

But he'd already made a big impression on Hollywood, with his slew of Hong Kong films like *The Killer, Hard Boiled*, and *A Better Tomorrow*, all character-driven shoot-'em-ups that had made a star of his regular lead actor, the debonair Chow Yun-fat. A year later, Nicolas Cage would pay due homage on the set of Woo's film *Face/Off*, by appearing on-set in shades, a fake moustache, and a slicked-back hairstyle. As the entire crew looked on, astonished, Cage walked up to Woo and flashed a wicked grin. "You like the new look?" he asked. "It's very Chow Yun-fat."

Looking for a hero

A flash-cut, to eight years later: Some 2,000 theatres across America have screened the latest hit film coming out of China. Opening at number one with a US$17.8 million grossing weekend, the movie was yet another martial arts spectacle, a period piece featuring sword-fighting warriors called *Hero*. And it carried the imprimatur of the genre's most unabashed fan: "Quentin Tarantino presents," preceded the credits. One simple line, but it had made a tremendous difference. It had brought people out to the theatres.

Tarantino, as Hollywood's most powerful director of cutting-edge movies, had validated it with the power of his own personal branding. "Making that association was very useful for getting the film out to an American audience," *Hero*'s director Zhang Yimou told the *New York Times*, gamely giving credit to the confluence of market forces shaping its success.

The story of *Hero*'s box-office success is in actuality the story of Asia's ascent in the West, with all its inscrutable complexities intact.

Zhang, previously known to most American moviegoers for his film *Raise the Red Lantern*, noted that he had kept Western audiences in mind while making the film – because he knew he would not be able to recoup the production costs through Chinese ticket sales alone. "I tried to get across themes that would be understood by a Western audience. There are elements that are purely Chinese, but I made an effort to keep a balance between the two." He cut 20 minutes from the original 2002 version that had been screened widely across Asia, to speed up the pace and make it more palatable for American audiences – on the advice, apparently, of Miramax, which distributed the film and covered nearly two-thirds of the US$30 million budget.

When Miramax did not release the film in 2003, tongues wagged that the company was not happy with Zhang's version. Miramax co-chairman Harvey Weinstein, however, wrote a guest column in the film industry trade journal *Variety*, to coincide with the 2004 US opening. He claimed it was planned all along – they'd held back the release in 2003 because they did not want to compete with Jackie Chan's martial arts film *Medallion* and also wanted to release it after Quentin Tarantino's two *Kill Bill* films, running trailers for *Hero* in the *Kill Bill Vol. 1* DVD and in the theatres prior to *Kill Bill Vol. 2*.

Additionally, Miramax had decided to deploy the big marketing push with "Quentin Tarantino presents," so as to draw interest from Tarantino's avid followers. The strategy apparently worked, though some critics noted that the US$17.8 million opening weekend occurred during a slow moviegoing time, on the cusp of summer going into fall. And, of course, there had been a precedent of sorts, a film called *Crouching Tiger, Hidden Dragon*, by the Taiwanese director Ang Lee. It had cost US$15 million and had sold US$128 million in tickets in the United States alone. "*Crouching Tiger* created an audience for this kind of film," admitted Zhang, since *Hero* fell into the exotic genre of *wuxia pian*, the Chinese way of fusing sword-fighting adrenaline with martial-arts flair.

Why else would American audiences want to see a lengthy epic set in the third century BC, the story of an assassin sent to kill the future Chinese emperor, Qin Shihuang, the man who had built the famous Great Wall and unified the country's many fiefdoms?

It is perhaps fitting that the West would take to Asia (and its film stars) within such a context, since the previous episodes of Asian exotica have all been akin to skirmishes between warring states. Since the death of Bruce Lee in 1973, so many male actors were saddled with the curse of following his long shadow and few survived. Lee's legacy is embedded in his screen persona, the tough guy who fights oppression for the sake of moral rectitude, the kind of icon that African-Americans and other minority groups adopted simply because he mirrored their own situations. His first two films, *The Big Boss* and *Fist of Fury*, remain classics for their depiction of Jacobean tragedies told through the Chinese way of enacting revenge – one man against many, defying all odds.

Interestingly, in January 2005 the National Society of Film Critics in the United States chose Zhang Yimou as best director of 2004, for *Hero* and *House of Flying Daggers* (both released in 2004 in the USA), once again setting the tone for how the West still prefers to see Asia: all awash in kung-fu and chop-socky, with some swordplay to boot. Otherwise, it's still all about Jackie Chan with his comedic ballet or the *Crouching Tiger* triumvirate of Chow Yun-fat, Michelle Yeoh, and Zhang Ziyi. The guys who like Chow for his John Woo movies remain a fervent minority, only one step removed from the geeks who remember Bruce Lee as Winslow Wong in the 1969 film *Marlowe* or Kato in television's *The Green Hornet* – bit-part, sidekick roles that Lee detested.

But in the field of celebrity iconography, there is much evidence suggesting that Asia is itself to blame for failing to elevate its stars. Why has this simply not happened, when so many American and European film critics have long discovered what the public at large is now only beginning to appreciate?

Lights, cameras, inaction!

John Powers, writing in *L.A. Weekly* about the debut of Wong Kar-wai's film *2046* at the Cannes Film Festival in 2004, noted how "Tony Leung, who moves with perfect grace, uses the camera to capture the most delicate effects and (take note, Sean Penn) understands that the most powerful gestures are often the quietest ... you should race online to get a DVD of his dazzling work in *Infernal Affairs* – he's one of the world's greatest movie stars, with all the casual glamour that implies." Small wonder that Brad Pitt reportedly yearned to play Leung's role in the American remake of *Infernal Affairs*, having already purchased the US rights for some US$1.75 million, with director Martin Scorsese attached to the project.

Evidence abounds that the West has long been infatuated with Asian pop culture. In 2004 Sarah Michelle Gellar (television's *Buffy the Vampire Slayer*) starred in *The Grudge*, the remake of the Japanese horror film *Ju-on* helmed by its original director, Takashi Shimizu. Southeast Asia has been a haven for filming since 1982, when Peter Weir and Mel Gibson made *The Year of Living Dangerously* (set in Indonesia), and Leonardo DiCaprio went to Thailand in 1999 for *The Beach*. Some of the better films, though, were known mostly (and sometimes only) in the art-house circles: Regis Wargnier's *Indochine*, Jean-Jacques Annaud's *The Lover* (both set in Vietnam) and John Boorman's *Beyond Rangoon* (with Malaysia doubling for Burma). There seems to exist a chasm between them and the likes of a star-heavy vehicle like *Anna and the King* (Jodie Foster and Chow Yun-fat in a remake of *The King and I*, with Malaysia doubling for Thailand).

None of these films made a star out of anyone who wasn't already one, nor did they make catch-phrases of the titles the way say, *Double Indemnity* or *Basic Instinct* did. And none of them did much to rescue the Hong Kong film industry from the crash of the late 1980s, even though the very words "Hong Kong action film" have become a marketing buzzword. To understand this failure is to understand the way the creation of celebrity works, in terms of the factors at play that make or break a cultural phenomenon.

On June 11, 2004, the *South China Morning Post* devoted a large feature with the headline "Light, camera, inaction" to analyzing this dilemma. ("Hong Kong's film industry could realise its true value if it worked with local merchandisers who are already stretching Hollywood's profits, analysts tell David Watkins," read the subtitle.) The piece riffed on about how so much of Hollywood's movie-related merchandise is actually made in either Hong Kong or China.

Rand Brenner, a former Warner Bros. licensing manager who'd gotten the ball rolling with *Batman* – one of the first movies to put the books, comics, and toys on the shelves even before the movie came out – addressed the annual Filmart conference the previous September, with the exhortation to Hong Kong to do more with its own movies.

"Trust is a huge part of it," Brenner conceded. "When I first started at Warner Bros., this was the central issue. The mentality was: 'These are our secrets. We can't let these out.' It took time to be able to integrate the whole idea of working in concert – that your manufacturers are part of your productions." One manifestation of this is in the field of computer games. Halle Berry, for instance, got tremendous mileage for endorsing the computer games released to promote *Catwoman*, even as the film itself bombed. The games and the merchandising they spawned kept her name in the limelight and put her on the covers of countless magazines in the summer of 2004.

But in the case of Hong Kong movies, there are three basic problems.

First, the economies of scale are massively different – the average computer game costs ten times the amount it takes to make a Hong Kong movie (unlike with a Hollywood movie, where the game costs a fraction of the budget). Second, rampant software piracy across Asia tends to dishearten game developers and manufacturers, since no one is ever sure of recouping their investment. And third, there is insufficient development time to create the games anyway, since most Hong Kong movies are made guerrilla-style – with barely any finished scripts before shooting; how can a game be created when no one knows how the script will even read?

The last is almost a rhetorical question, but it actually underscores the difference in mindset between East and West. Particularly in America, marketers in entertainment companies have fully acknowledged the potential of brand power and have harnessed the means to make this a reality. In Asia, it seems, everyone is waiting for a Quentin Tarantino to pick up the cudgel and spread the gospel.

"Marketing spend will have to be tailored according to market size, in order to be justifiable, especially with the China market opening up," noted Eric Yeo, the film columnist for Malaysia's largest-selling Chinese-language daily newspaper, *Sin Chew Daily*. "I foresee that marketing and promotions for celebrities will be big in scale, though it's not fair to compare between the East and the West. The cultures, celebrity requirements and the fans' acceptance levels are not the same. I still think we have a lot to learn from the West. They have been doing this way ahead of us for many years."

Yeo, who says his own favorite Asian movie stars are Tony Leung and Anthony Wong ("because they are versatile and have their own style") lamented the current slate of stars in the international spotlight. "Chow Yun-fat has not been a breakthrough because he is stuck in the same mold, and Jackie Chan's Hollywood career has almost come to an end. American audiences are finding that he is doing the same stunts over and over again, and the result is that his recent films like *Tuxedo*, *The Medallion* and *Around the World in 80 Days* were all flops. Tony Leung is not an action star, so he won't get mass attention. Jet Li stands a chance, but he lacks a clear identity."

What of Michelle Yeoh and her television ads, where she served as the pitchperson for Malaysian tourism? "There's only one place I call home: Malaysia. Truly Asia," quipped the former beauty queen (Miss Malaysia 1983), on behalf of her home country of 25 million people, even as most people know her usual home to be in the swank Peak district of Hong Kong, the city where her film career began in 1985.

"I personally do not agree that she should be a Malaysian 'brand'," Yeo averred, speaking as a Malaysian too. "She does not really live in Malaysia, she contributes nothing to Malaysia, and she became an internationally known star because of a James Bond film seven years ago but this has nothing to do with Malaysia. If she had made a Malaysian film that became an international box office blockbuster, then that's a different thing. She is just a promotional vehicle."

Wine, women, songs

"There's nothing like Lindemans shared among friends," runs the sanguine ad tagline, with Jackie Chan's blissful visage shot by photographer Russel Wong. Chan actually drinks what he endorses – Lindemans wines, from Karadoc in the state of Victoria, in Australia, self-professed "winemakers since 1843" – and he is also a wine collector, Wong noted.

Chan continues to tout the virtues of his native land as the official pitchman for Hong Kong tourism. "Jackie really loves Hong Kong, and if he could he would do those commercials for free," Wong said, having worked closely with Chan for many years. Chan now also has his own clothing line, and there are many among his adoring public who perceive him as an affable family man.

Luckily for Chan, he has never emulated other Hong Kong film stars like Andy Lau and the late Leslie Cheung – those opting for a dual career, as actor and singer. In contrast to film stars, pop singers are more craftily "made" in Asia. Most record producers in the United States would blanch at the thought of such prolific output – Hong Kong's most acclaimed singer, for instance, is Sammi Cheng, who launched her "Cantopop" singing career in 1992 and now, at the age of 31, has cut 30 solo albums and starred in 15 movies. She also appeared in a series of ad campaigns for SK-II, a female skin-lightening cream. In Hong Kong, such prolific output is par for the course. Talent scouts sign girls as young as 14, and groom them into starlets, with promises of multiple-album contracts and fame.

"Most of them don't know how to sing, and the agents teach them how," explained one former agent, Garvid Cheng, who did just that for World Star Music International, a label known for reviving the flagging careers of one-time Asian icons like the 1980s pop idol Frances Yip. Cheng spoke to the *Asian Wall Street Journal* in May 2004, in an article on the plight of the Hong Kong actress/singer hyphenate called "Starlets Make a Stand."

The story was a revealing one, noting the often brief careers of many Hong Kong female stars: Linda Lin Dai, the "Doris Day of

Hong Kong," who achieved fame in the late 1950s (and committed suicide in 1964); Cherie Chung, the "Elizabeth Taylor of Hong Kong," a big star in the 1980s who dropped out at the height of her success in 1991 (to marry an advertising executive); Brigitte Lin, a firm favorite among *wuxi* fans and the star of many kung-fu classics, who quit in 1994 (to become a wife and mother, after marrying Esprit Holdings boss Michael Ying).

Such is the "ideal" for most Hong Kong starlets: Hang on for ten years, marry a rich man, and retire by 30.

"Women are seen as a short-term investment," disclosed John Chong, executive director of the commercial production house Media Asia, interviewed in the same *Asian Wall Street Journal* article. "In our industry, we groom actors for ten years, but we groom an actress for two months." Media Asia now has its own talent agency, which represents such established stars as the singer/actor Andy Lau, Tony Leung's nemesis in *Infernal Affairs*, who has acted in a staggering 114 films in 21 years.

Maggie Cheung, who received rave notices for her role in *Hero*, remains one of the more visible stars to emerge from the Hong Kong system. Best known for her roles in Wong Kar-wai's early films (*As Tears Go By, Days of Being Wild*), she was born in Hong Kong but bred in England, and came to the attention of Western audiences via Wayne Wang's 1997 film *Chinese Box*. Like Michelle Yeoh, she came into acting after a run of beauty pageants; Cheung was the 1983 Miss Hong Kong runner-up, but also the Miss Photogenic winner – a significant fact, since she was then breaking into commercials.

"I used Maggie in the first-ever commercial she ever did, for McDonald's," recalled Hans Ebert, then the creative director at DDB Needham Hong Kong (and now the executive director of EMI Music Southeast Asia). "I paid her HK$300 and she worked two days. She was 17, in Hong Kong from London, and she worked on four McDonald's commercials in Hong Kong, in one month.

"I knew right away. I just knew that this girl was going to be a star. The fact that she is now considered the 'Catherine Deneuve of Asia' – I'm not really surprised. Production houses always come and give you videotapes with 12 or 15 girls, and Maggie was one of the girls. She had not been in anything at the time. Nothing. This was 1978."

His recollection remains vivid, since she'd apparently made quite an impression on him. "She was very cute, she had this really cute Cockney accent. That commercial for McDonald's had to do with being able to dance. She had a sense of rhythm. And she photographed well, which was good because she had three other commercials to do. The commercial eventually won a Clio in New York."

But in recent years, Cheung has shied from the limelight and largely rebuffed the Hong Kong press (especially after some private love letters she'd written to an American-Chinese beau were somehow published in a tabloid). "I'm not ambitious enough to find an agent in Hollywood and try my luck there," she told writer J. H. Huang, in *Elle Singapore*, February 2000. "I really want things to come to me, and choose from there." Perhaps the stoic, introspective Asian in her speaks for the rest of her kin, preferring sanity over stardom. Asian celebrityhood, on the world stage, might be better off staying that way.

Bollywood blues

Russel Wong, who shot Cheung on the set of Zhang Yimou's *Hero*, understands the creation of celebrity all too well, having acquired a reputation as Asia's foremost celebrity portrait photographer. His work hasn't appeared merely on those Jackie Chan ads for Lindemans wines; his photos have graced numerous magazine covers, including stunning portraits of Bollywood star Aishwarya Rai for *Time* magazine's Asian edition and Zhang Ziyi, in aerial swordfighting glory, for *Premiere* magazine's Japanese edition.

The Rai shoot for *Time* was set in one of the most exotic of Asian locales – the Aguada Hermitage, at the Fort Aguada Beach Resort in Goa. "Before I shot her, I asked the make-up artist to avoid the Bollywood look, with the heavy eyeliner," he recalled. "I thought, why would you want to use heavy eyeliner to cover and camouflage her eyes when she has the most beautiful eyes in the world? In my view, if I see that the eyes have been drawn too heavy, I'll have them water it down. So I asked her if that would be okay and she said, 'Fine.'

"It gave her a new look, a fresher look, different from what everyone else has seen of her. So that's my input. I wanted to strip down all that make-up and show her eyes, to how beautiful she is by altering the make-up. And her clothes too, so she would not be wearing something fanciful. It should be something simple, so I put her in a black Armani dress."

Permission must always be sought directly from the subject, not the stylist. "She can veto the stylist," Wong noted. "The make-up is going to be put on her in the end, anyway, but there has to be some explaining – you have to tell them why. What's the concept, what's the direction, why you want to try something different."

The clothes for the shoot were chosen by Wong. "I picked them. She gave me a list of designers that she liked. And so I knew who to choose, so that whatever she wore would at least be within the zone that she felt comfortable with. It's a psychological thing. If they're going to wear a designer they don't like, they're going to say, 'I hate the clothes.' I have also found sometimes, there's only so far you can push. Sometimes, there is politics involved, if the make-up artist's best friend or her sister is there working too. You can't tell her family member that her make-up is bad or that her styling sucks!"

All photographers immersed in celebrity imaging have to skirt a fine line, striking a delicate balance between person and the persona. Clothes inevitably become an extension of persona, becoming part of the ploy by which a person exudes glamour. "I always shoot to the person," Wong disclosed. "To me, the person has got to look good. The clothes, I'm not as concerned about. I think that if the person will look good, the product will look good. How many times do you see an ad or a magazine cover and you'll go, 'Wow, she looks great!' You never say, 'The outfit looks great! And, by the way, she's kind of nice.' Even in an ad, you will say, 'She looks great!' And then, by the way, 'Oh, it's a Louis Vuitton ad.'

"Because it's the person who carries it and wears it – that's what you pay for. If she doesn't have a certain charm or a certain charisma, or she just doesn't look good, the product will look bad. Even though it's the same bag or the same outfit."

With Aishwarya Rai, Wong's portraits conveyed the message that her star was ascendant ("Aishwarya Rai leads the invasion as Bollywood goes global and gets hip," read the *Time* coverline). Her look was self-contained and projected a quiet confidence, almost as if to say she could well be a break-out star any day now.

Nevertheless, Bollywood's charms have made inroads to the West but have not quite ensnared a universal mindshare. India's film industry is vast – it makes more than 1,000 films a year, with Bollywood itself accounting for 800 of these (generating some US$450 million annually in ticket sales). For all its passions and undulations, the Bollywood film genre remains a cult taste. Salman Khan, Sanjay Dutt, and Amitabh Bachchan (as well as his son Abhishek) have yet to make the cross-cultural leap equivalent to Jackie Chan, Jet Li, and Bruce Lee; most moviegoers know more about the Jennifer Lopez/ Ben Affleck fiasco (or the Jennifer Garner/Ben Affleck fiasco-to-be) than all the rumours surrounding Aishwarya Rai and her beau Vivek Oberoi.

And Malika Sherawat, the sultry star of Jackie Chan's newest film *The Myth*, may call herself "box office Viagra," but the ultimate truth is that the most famous Indian person in the film world today is of Hollywood and not Bollywood: the director M. Night Shyamalan, who came to the fore with *The Sixth Sense* in 1999 and has since built himself a reputation as the Alfred Hitchcock of our time.

"Bollywood cinema speaks to *deshis*" – Indian people from South Asia – "as if they are members of a secret club." That's the view of Vinita Ramani, a Mumbai-born writer who has analyzed Indian cinema for *Raj Palta*, the South-Asian Canadian newspaper. "It is a feeling of 'home,' packaged in a sprawling, three-hour, genre-splicing film. And Bollywood films have so much panache, style and excessiveness that it seems like unbridled hedonism; there's pleasure to be found in that as well as money to be made. It may not be a panacea for much of its below-poverty-line audience in India, but it provides some respite from the daily grind."

Ramani, deconstructing the genre in an article called "Boom-boom Bollywood" (published in *Harper's Bazaar Singapore* in October 2002), praised South Asian musical talents such as the band Asian Dub Foundation and also cited the presence of cinema complexes like the India Movie Centre and the Naz 8 in San Francisco, a city with 100,000 South Asians. The former, a six-screen cineplex, even sells Indian snacks to moviegoers who are greeted by sari-clad concessionaires. The latter is a 1,860-seat theatre, located in the East Bay enclave of Fremont, with a beauty salon-cum-sari store called Beauty Plus and a restaurant called Masala Grill next door.

Only three Indian films have ever been nominated for Oscars in the Best Foreign Film category (*Mother India, Salaam Bombay!* and *Lagaan*) while *Bend It Like Beckham*, a 2002 film directed by Gurinder Chadha about the plight of young Indian women in England dreaming of soccer stardom, emerged as an unlikely independent hit. *Bend It Like Beckham* also showcased the then-unknown talents of a young English actress named Keira Knightley, who in a space of a mere few years, became one of the most highly-hyped new faces of Hollywood.

Herein lay a pointed metaphor: Knightley isn't Indian at all, but a certain infatuation with her has already begun (thanks to her visibility, playing opposite Johnny Depp in *Pirates of the Caribbean: The Curse of the Black Pearl*, and in the medieval epic *Arthur*), while Indian beauties like Priyanka Chopra, Lara Dutta, and Sushmita Sen still remain unknown to the outside world. Perhaps one of them could have been cast in the Merchant/Ivory film *The Goddess* instead of the American rock star Tina Turner, whose casting as the Hindu goddess Shakti angered religious groups in India? Perhaps the world at large isn't ready for an Indian movie superstar.

"Better to rule in India than to serve in Hollywood," the Bollywood icon Shah Rukh Khan once said, though some would decry it as sour grapes. Could one imagine, say, Bruce Lee saying the same thing? Lee, all his biographers agree, made no bones about his ambitions – he wanted to rule the world. The fact remains that he was the man who single-handedly popularized kung-fu. Hong Kong cinema was merely the vehicle for his towering genius. He didn't need

Quentin Tarantino back then, not with students and devotees like Steve McQueen and Chuck Norris, who promoted him as a brand most eloquently.

Decades from now, surely nobody will say the same of William Hung, the *American Idol* cast-off who scored a bizarre, gimmicky hit with his off-key rendition of Ricky Martin's "She Bangs," and then scored a record deal. The most ironic of his achievements, however, has been in "inspiring" countless would-be singers (hence the title of Hung's debut album, *Inspiration*) – to emulate his tuneless crooning on copycat idol contests, in hopes of being catapulted to fame too.

Hung out to dry

"William Hung, I think, is a disgrace to Asians," proclaimed EMI's Hans Ebert. "What was a joke has now become, I think, an insult to Asians. It just plays to American audiences who think that Asians have buck teeth and can't dance and are bad lovers. He's not in on the joke, but I think actually the worst part is that his parents are part of this and I think that's really, really sad. They're typical Hong Kong, they've made this kid of theirs into a cartoon character and they want people to pay for this. I feel sorry for William Hung, but I'm pissed off at his parents."

However, he's at a loss to explain why Asian singers have generally failed to catch on in the West. Sony Music had tried with the Hong Kong-born, Chinese-American singer CoCo Lee and the sultry Indonesian chanteuse Anggun Sasmi, but both failed to ignite outside Asia with their albums.

Then there was the sassy songstress Tata Young from Thailand, whose previous claim to fame was as the sometime-girlfriend of tennis sensation Paradorn Srichaphan. Young (who was actually named after India's Tata, as in the auto maker Tata Motors) endured a media blitz with her 2004 hit song "Sexy, Naughty, Bitchy," which aroused the ire of the Thai Ministry of Culture. Naturally, it helped her sell more records than she might have done unaided, proving that controversy can be the best kind of sales tool. "We told the radio stations here that in the past, there were things like Meredith Brooks's hit song 'Bitch' and there were no problems with that at all," said Kieven Yim, Director of Strategic Marketing at Sony BMG Music, in Hong Kong. "One station here picked up the Tata Young song and the next thing I knew, all the other stations were playing it! Sometimes all you need is one station to start the ball rolling."

CoCo Lee's problem, some theorized, was that she sounded much too much like Mariah Carey. Asian celebrities generally lack the conviction to present a unique individual voice. "We have always been looking to the West and so we will always be second-best," Russel Wong noted. "I don't know if confidence is the right word, but very few Asian celebrities have it. They always second-guess, they have to turn to the stylist or their hair or their make-up people to tell them what looks nice on them. I see a lot of that happening.

"I find the more mature and more confident, tried-and-tested celebrities are the ones who will assert themselves in wearing only what they would feel comfortable with. A good example is Michelle Yeoh. I know dresses and outfits are always being thrown at her, for shows and events that she attends. I've gone to shoot her and the whole room is stacked full of clothes that have been given to her. But she usually ends up wearing only what she is comfortable with, and sometimes it's her own clothes. It's not about clout. It's about just being confident about yourself and not needing that whole 'designer injection.'"

In Asia, the very idea of fame harkens back to Bruce Lee, who didn't care what you thought of his haircut or his snarling, sneering way of luring opponents to their doom. He was, after all, Lee Sui-Lung, Lee the "Little Dragon". Jackie Chan resisted being cast as the successor to Bruce Lee, having decided that he would make his own mark with his unique style of action/comedy, even as he readily paid tribute to Bruce for paving the way.

"Without him, I don't think that anyone would ever have heard of Jackie Chan," Chan admitted in his autobiography, *I Am Jackie Chan: My life in action*, published in 1998. But a complex nexus of forces were at work, not least of all his long-time manager Willie Chan, who co-created the Jackie Chan myth by negotiating all the critical deals: a multi-million dollar contract with Golden Harvest (the very studio of Bruce Lee's films) and the Hollywood crossover-hit films – *Rumble in the Bronx* (the very first Hong Kong film to hit number one at the US box office, with a US$9.8 million opening weekend,) and the two *Rush Hour* movies (with *Rush Hour 3* apparently on the way).

"There's a price to pay for success," Jackie recalled Willie advising him, in the same autobiography. "The bigger you get, the more pieces of you people want. Now, there's a secret to dealing with the media. All you have to do is plan out in advance what you want to say. We'll work out all the questions that they might possibly ask, and figure out answers for them."

Second-guessing the answers may be the best strategy any celebrity needs to perfect, in order to stay on-brand. But Asia can still learn something from the West – the ability to replace stoicism with spontaneity, and rise to the occasion. Bruce Lee and Jackie Chan remain the only ones who have really succeeded, if one doesn't count William Hung. People want to see their idols charged-up and ready to pump up the volume, whether or not they're presented by Quentin Tarantino.

Russel Wong

Russel Wong is best-known as a portrait photographer of Asian celebrities. His work has been on the covers of *Time*, *Premiere*, and *Vogue*, featuring the likes of Jackie Chan, Chow Yun-fat, Zhang Ziyi, Faye Wong, and Aishwarya Rai, and he has also shot Jet Li, Joan Chen, Andy Lau, Christy Chung, Maggie Cheung, and Michelle Yeoh. Formerly based in Los Angeles, he now works from both his native Singapore and film locations in Hong Kong and China.

When you are shooting a celebrity, are you conscious of the fact that you are shooting a celebrity?

Of course. That's why you think about the styling and the image, which magazines the photos are going to be placed, and what clothes they put on. You are very conscious of this. They will ask you questions like, "What clothes are you going to put me in?" and "What's the shot going to be?" Or they'll say to you, "This is my good side," so that you will shoot from that side. You're constantly being reminded that they are celebrities.

What is your approach to shooting a celebrity, given that you're actually selling a person as a brand?

I always shoot to the person. To me, the person has got to look good. The clothes, I don't care about as much. I think that if the person will look good, the product will look good. How many times do you see an ad or a magazine cover and you'll go, "Wow, she looks great." You never say, "The outfit looks great and, by the way, she's kind of nice." Even in an ad, you will say, "She looks great!" And, by the way, "Oh, it's a Louis Vuitton ad." Because it's the person who carries it and wears it. That's what you pay for.

How is shooting Asian celebrities different from shooting Western celebrities?

I think that the packaging is different. The packaging of Asian celebrities is more manufactured than with Western celebrities, in the sense that sometimes they're wearing clothes that they wouldn't even own. They wouldn't go out to shop for these things. It's manufactured because it's not a personal style. There is more individuality, to me, in the West. They can wear street clothes with no labels, whereas the Asian market is so label-driven.

How is this manifested in the photos you take?

If a new designer has a new line out, everyone's given the same outfit. So there's a press rack that primarily rotates and, for a particular season, everyone will wear that. Flip through the Asian magazines and you'll see different celebrities wearing the same outfits. To me, this is ridiculous, because the celebrities are not wearing the clothes as much as the clothes are wearing them. Remember the time that Sharon Stone went to the Oscars and wore a Gap T-shirt? Do you honestly think most Asian celebrities would do that? I don't think so.

Do you think this is just "Asian thinking"?

Maybe. They are so label-driven and so name-conscious, so conformist in that way. Because we always looked to British and French *Vogue*, and we drew from that because they represented the "fashion mecca" – you could call it a very "colonial" mentality. Also, I don't know if confidence is the right word, but very few Asian celebrities have it. Faye Wong is one of the few who has her own individual style. And I think Michelle Yeoh is very stylish. She's not like your normal, girl-next-door. She can be a bit boyish – cool and chic, in jeans – and look great in it. She has a certain edge.

Where you do think Chinese film celebrity is heading?

Well, a country like China with a population of 1.4 billion has produced only two major film stars – Gong Li and Zhang Ziyi. Why is this? Interesting, isn't it?

7
Brit-Pop and the Boom-Boomerang: For the Love of Britney and Kylie

They're literally oceans apart, separated by more than a decade, and still tilling the fields of the terminally young. Britney Spears is 22 and Kylie Minogue is 36, and the difference is only startling when you realize one salient fact: When Kylie made her mark on the music world with her debut album in 1988, she was the same age as Britney when the latter released her third album.

Kids these days, they grow up so fast.

The young ex-Mouseketeer from Louisiana had already established her presence the year before, when her album *Oops! ... I Did It Again* broke the record for first-week sales by a single female artist on the *Billboard* chart. It entered the chart at number 1 and sold an astonishing 1.319 million copies that first week alone. (The previous record was held by Alanis Morissette, with a relatively paltry 469,054 copies sold in its first week for *Supposed Former Infatuation Junkie*.) It even broke the record for most units sold by a female artist in any one week. (The previous record was Mariah Carey, whose album *Daydream* sold 759,959 in the week of Christmas 1995.)

Kylie has never tasted that level of success in the United States, though her fans will attest that she is a huge star in the rest of the world, with the same eyeball rolling aplomb that they would tell Americans that football is not soccer and they're missing out on the world's most popular sport.

Britney's world is not quite the same as Kylie's, although on the level of celebrity and glamour they certainly intersect. The place where they meet is unquestionably intriguing to anyone puzzled over the creation of celebrity brands, since both deal in what many critics would call the distinctly kitsch realm of disposable pop music. The one thing they have in common is a relentless drive to maintain their public profile. In their version of show business, image is everything.

Oh, to be young and blonde and sexy! That's the message they both send out, though Kylie had a quite a headstart on Britney, and boasts an appeal squarely locked on a somewhat different demographic segment – gay men, as opposed to merely teenage girls, much of this attributed to the aesthetic brilliance of her

145

creative director William Baker, gay himself (of course) and the author of the lavish coffee-table book *Kylie: La La La,* published in 2002, no doubt already on the bookshelf of every self-respecting fashion stylist.

"Kylie is a great canvas on which to experiment," Baker told Australian *Vogue*, in a cover story on Kylie in May 2003. "She does the avant-garde but at the same time she has incredible mass appeal. Very few people can combine the two. Even Madonna doesn't do it as successfully as Kylie. I mean, Madonna can be so confronting that she provokes quite an extreme response, whereas Kylie has become the object of affection."

Choice words, though the kind of response she has elicited might be considered extreme in certain cultures. Those gold hot pants displaying her suggestively bare bottom, made infamous in her "Spinning Around" video, have not played the same way to American audiences. Committing suicide in a bathtub, as Britney did in her controversial "Everytime" video (supposedly about her doomed relationship with ex-beau Justin Timberlake), seemed to push more buttons in the collective psyche. Interestingly, that same month in 2004, the number one single in Kylie's native Australia was … Britney Spears's "Everything."

Is there some kind of culture clash afoot, that might explain the differences between these two women? William Baker actually attributes Kylie's popularity to the fact that she comes from Melbourne, Australia. "She's like sunshine. She exudes it. Everything about Australia is embodied within her because she's so easygoing and so … sunny." (Of course, many Englishmen might say that anyway about Australia, even if Melbourne gets more rain than most cities Down Under.) Britney, on the other hand, hails from small-town Kentwood, Louisiana (population 2,600), and oozes the down-home charm of the American South. Her sunny disposition is that of the college-sweetheart archetype, but garnished with the sassy spirit of the cheerleader who might (and only might) have sex with the quarterback.

It represents powerful branding, and it's a metaphor that doesn't exist in soccer.

Terrifico!

"The press can talk about my clothes, talk about my hair, anything, and I don't care. Seriously. Sometimes I'll wear retarded things just to see what they'll say." That was Britney, talking to *Rolling Stone* at the end of 2001. "Once you label yourself a role model, people start judging you, saying you should be this way or that way. And I do not want that at all."

But what about allegations that she's a manufactured entity? "That's just stupid. They think that people come in and put my clothes together or put me together? I come up with the concepts for all of my tour ideas, all of my videos. When I first got signed to the record label, honestly, I was 16 years old – I didn't know what I was doing. For my first photo shoot, I remember they even got a certain hair person to come in and do my hair, and they totally whacked my hair up. And I was pissed." They wanted her to wear stuff she didn't like, too. "Little-girl clothes. Just like, stuff from the Gap."

No word has emerged from Gap about those comments, especially since it prides itself as a casual clothier that prefers to use less prominent, more edgy music stars like Joss Stone and Taryn Manning in its ads. Britney, clearly, considered herself in a different league. She endorsed Skechers, but her own sneakers were candy-pink and jewel-encrusted. She was photographed in Milan wearing a US$23,000 rainbow-colored sequinned gown in the company of its designer, Donatella Versace. "Terrifico! I want everything," she said as she wriggled and giggled at the after-show party for the Milan Spring–Summer 2003 collections, as reported by the ever-observant fashion critic Suzy Menkes in the *International Herald Tribune*. That was in October 2002, just prior to ending her six-month sabbatical and entering the studio again to record her third album *In The Zone*.

At that juncture in time, Kylie had already released eight studio albums and scored 38 hit singles worldwide. Her single "Can't Get You Out of My Head" from the most recent album, *Fever*, had made number one in almost every territory that it was released. What Kylie had essentially done with that was make her long-awaited "come-back," after a dry spell.

Her net worth is estimated at US$22.5 million, and who remembers her fallow years now? She had five sell-out world tours, with critically acclaimed performances at the 1992 Lennon Memorial Concert in Liverpool and, in her native Melbourne, the opening of Mushroom Records' 25th anniversary concert and the opening of the Fox Studios complex in 1998. Then she wowed them at the closing ceremony of the 2000 Olympic Games in Sydney, all gussied up in a pink showgirl uniform complete with feathered head-dress, performing Abba's "Dancing Queen" in front of a four-billion audience.

"It confirmed her transformation into the new Kylie Minogue," wrote authors Jenny Stanley-Clarke and Nigel Goodall in their unabashedly worshipful 2002 biography *Kylie Naked*, which opened with an epigraph from Kylie herself: "I don't have to try to be a sex bomb, I am one!" Her record sales were already hovering at 50 million sold when she launched her own line of lingerie called Love Kylie, in 2000, featuring lacy boudoir-style bras and pastel-pretty panties, flirty slips and black slithery negligées with satin bows – the very thing one would expect from a sophisticated sex kitten.

The lingerie line represented a remarkable branding opportunity and a very congruent use of brand extension, since it reflects her onstage demeanour. Her iconic image was used to complement her apparel marketing.

Britney, almost as if she needed to counter that, posed in black silk and lace corsets (and other black silk and lacy things) created by Tom Ford for Gucci (just before he left Gucci) – the very same month she showed up at the MTV Video Music awards in 2003 dressed to resemble Madonna in "Like a Virgin" and then famously kissed the former Material Girl herself (smack-dab on the mouth, prompting speculation: "Was there tongue?"). Britney's total record sales, at that time, were estimated in the region of 26 million – about half of Kylie's. However, Kylie had enjoyed a ten-year head-start; her first album came out in 1988 (whereas Britney did not even start recording till 1998), and hers was a trajectory full of watershed events.

The girl from *Neighbours*

She was bound to bounce back, since "kylie" is the native Australian word for "boomerang." Born Kylie Ann Minogue on May 28, 1968 at Bethlehem Hospital in Melbourne, she was singing to Abba songs at age 8, using a broom handle for a microphone. At age 10, she experienced her first musical epiphany – she saw *Grease*, the 1977 film, and was captivated by Olivia Newton-John's performance of "You're the One That I Want." She wanted to be Olivia, performing up there with John Travolta. Then, as all Australians know, Kylie appeared on their pop culture compass when she was 17, landing the part of Charlene Mitchell, the headstrong girl in the television soap opera *Neighbours*. Chosen from 40 other girls, Kylie starred in the series from February 1986 to June 1988.

But her first real taste of celebrity creation took place in 1986, and it was devised by Bryan Walsh, the show's head publicist.

Kylie and her co-star, Jason Donovan, were already attracting a strong cult following (despite the presence of another actor in the ensemble who would later make it big too – Guy Pearce, star of the films *LA Confidential* and *Memento*), but Walsh believed in "direct persuasion": He organized promotional events at shopping malls in Sydney, aimed at getting press from the influential media outlets there. He had a film crew shoot footage of the massive crowds at these events and sent the copies of the tapes out to newspapers and magazines with a note explaining why these thousands of people at the malls were "rioting everywhere" that Kylie and Jason went.

This took a fateful turn when the storyline called for the couple's first screen kiss on an isolated beach. The *Daily Mirror* ran a front-page headline that read: "TV Shock: Teen Sex on TV Tonight." Of course, there was no sex at all, merely a kiss, but all the Sydney newspapers picked up on it. The power of celebrity kicked in, and Kylie and Jason made the cover of the influential Australian magazine *TV Week*.

The hoopla in Australia resulted in one significant spin-off effect – it aroused interest in the UK, and so *Neighbours* made its debut on

British television the same year, in October 1986. It became a runaway success due in part to the fact that Kylie and Jason were, by that time, lovers offscreen as well. Stanley-Clarke and Goodall, in their Kylie biography, noted that "exactly what made Charlene such compulsive viewing is still a mystery. Kylie couldn't understand it either – she was a mystified as anyone." Kylie's own best theory was that Charlene is "an average teenager who has problems with her boyfriend and with getting a career started. She's a bit of a rebel and they probably relate to that."

Nice enough if a tad maudlin, as all TV soaps are wont to be. However, Kylie would then reach the zenith of her small-screen fame through yet another Bryan Walsh creation. The time had come for Charlene and Scott to get married. Even *Time* magazine in Australia fell for it, with a heart-shaped photo of Kylie and Jason on its cover, in anticipation of the big episode. On the morning before the episode aired, Walsh organized a wedding breakfast staged at a suburban shopping mall in Sydney. Four thousand fans showed up. People were injured and hospitalized for treatment, and a visibly flustered Kylie and Jason were chaperoned away. It seemed entirely manufactured for the tabloids, yet it was no small accident, since it was at this very juncture that Kylie's metamorphosis from soap star to pop star began.

The official legend runs something like this: She appeared at a benefit concert for a footy (Australian Rules football) team, where she performed a duet with local actor Jon Waters. The song was "I Got You Babe" – the Sonny and Cher 1965 hit – and it received such applause that the audience demanded an encore. Kylie then got up and sang "The Loco-Motion," the 1962 Little Eva dance classic penned by Carole King and Gerry Goffin, and stunned everyone. She then recorded the song as a single and it made number one on the Australian record charts. This was July 1987, just two weeks after the *Neighbours* wedding episode had aired. Fame was fresh in the air.

Her rendition of "The Loco-Motion" became the biggest-selling single of the 1980s in Australia, and to this day remains the biggest-selling single in the history of the Mushroom Records label.

150

Amanda Pelham, the promotions manager at Mushroom Records, was largely credited for Minogue's signing – she'd listened to Kylie's demo tape and had championed it. The idea was hers, to release a single of "The Loco-Motion" right after the television wedding of Kylie and Jason – timing is everything, after all. She was proved correct; by November 1987, Kylie's version of "The Loco-Motion" had made number one in Hong Kong and New Zealand, having already hit number one in Australia and maintained that same position for two months. Mushroom realized they had a potential major star on their hands.

After Kylie's second recording, "I Should Be So Lucky" hit number one in both the UK and Australia, people began literally cashing in on her celebrity. (The song would eventually become number one in 18 countries.) An Australian traveler in Bali spied a photo adorning his hotel wall – it was of Kylie and Jason together, taken a year earlier when they'd vacationed in Bali, and Kylie was (as is the fashion on beaches in Bali) posing topless. The man swiped the photo and sold it for A$2,000, and it was published in all the Australian newspapers.

This single deed unwittingly fed the flames of Kylie's fledgling celebrity – because it called into question her supposedly wholesome image in Neighbours. It worked – she swept the 1988 Logie awards (the Australian Emmys), winning four awards, including "Most Popular Actress" for the second year in a row and the "Golden Logie" for "Most Popular Personality on Australian Television."

Kylie's debut album also earned her an entry in the Guinness Book of Records – as "youngest female soloist to have a number one British album." By the end of that year, the British press raved about how Kylie had moved from earning £150 per Neighbours episode to 10,000 pounds for personal appearances. She had sold £25 million worth of records in 12 months since the beginning of 1988, and her personal income was estimated at £5 million

Her biggest coup unquestionably occurred in January 1998, when she hired William Baker as her stylist. They had met a few years earlier, when she visited the designer Vivienne Westwood's fashion store in London. (Baker was then a student working part-time for

Westwood, and he quit to work full-time for Kylie.) "I had had absolutely no styling experience before," Baker recalled, "but I had kind of been fascinated with her for some time, ever since I saw her doing the ironing in the 'What Do I Have to Do' clip. It was strange, but I just felt drawn to her. She came into the store. I leapt from behind the counter and bombarded her with ideas and somehow persuaded her to go for a coffee." Later that year, Baker and Kylie co-designed the glamorously kitsch out for her concert tour, and his own career was off to a flying start.

A crucial element of the Kylie Minogue mythology is her sense of spirited exhibitionism, as demonstrated by the "Spinning Around" video in which she pranced around in suggestively short hot pants. Kylie, in many an interview, charmingly downplayed it, by blaming it on a girlfriend who had picked up the pants for 50 pence from a London flea market. But a confluence of events is often needed to make history, and this was no exception.

The "Spinning Around" video came out the same month that *GQ* magazine in the UK published its July issue, featuring a now-infamous photo of Kylie hitching up her skirt on a tennis court and scratching her bare bottom in front of the net. (It was ostensibly a tribute to the famous 1970s Athena poster, of a knickerless tennis player.) Kylie made a public statement, stating she wore panties for the shoot and the magazine had airbrushed them out.

Her management surely knew about it, especially since her manager Terry Blamey had copyright control over all her images. Later, Kylie said, "I had no idea that after the video came out, the tabloids would be writing about my bum for a week." A quotable quote, if there ever was one, though stylist William Baker himself said it better: "It's kind of a sexy song and wanted like a clubby feel and those hot pants were just kind of perfect. And the video was like a showcase for Kylie's bum really."

Was this manufactured controversy, made to look like an "accident"? No one is entirely sure, and that's the sheer beauty of it: In hindsight, it simply "became" part of the Kylie Minogue "comeback" campaign. Such is the stuff of pop culture, rendering some stars unfathomably irresistible.

Glad to be gay

Gay men have gone ga-ga, ever since Kylie did a drag queen imper-sonation in the video for her song "What Do I Have to Do?" Even her stylist William Baker rhapsodizes, in his book *Kylie: La La La*, "The shot where she is ironing, dressed in a Mugler version of a French maid's outfit, hurling the iron back and forth with more make-up on than Boy George, Marilyn and Pete Burns put together, remains my all-time favorite image of her, glamorising the most mundane of household chores."

Perhaps all gay men tend to swoon over such camp and kitsch, in ways that the straight world cannot fathom. And they are given to paroxysms of unfettered delight over the way she wiggled her butt in those gold hot pants, too. "By the end of the shoot, after so much sliding and grinding," Baker recalls, "most of the lamé had worn off the fifty-pence wonders, revealing two perfect circles of the white fabric base of the butt cheeks."

"They became a national obsession, bestowing upon her bottom a celebrity all its own," Baker swooned. "If Warhol were alive, her bottom would surely have been the subject of one of his portraits, inspired by repetition of its image and mass-marketing of idols and icons. Her bum became an icon and the endless debate about it has developed a life of its very own."

Indeed, Warhol's semiotic emphasis on the repetition of images is one that Kylie's publicity manual adopted, and it had played a major role in her success. Warhol had correctly guessed that the time would come when we would want our celebrity images repeated, over and over, like his proverbial Campbell's soup cans or his Marilyn Monroe images. Kylie herself acknowledged, in Baker's book, her attitude towards the whole subject. "I was more or less adopted by my gay audience. In fact, I was possibly the last to know. In the early 1990s, The Albury on Sydney's Oxford Street hosted a 'Kylie night' every Sunday. This was the first time I had heard of a 'Kylie Drag Show.'

"I don't like to analyse our relationship too much as it is what it is, and it's wonderful, but I think they related to my initial struggle to be accepted as myself and then to survive. Later still, my wrestles with contradiction. Not to mention my penchant for all things pink and showgirl."

Mega-stardom in America has eluded her, however, and no one knows exactly why. Kylie's biggest success in the United States occurred in 2002, when her album *Fever* peaked at number three on the *Billboard* albums chart and its single "Can't Get You Out of My Head" went up to number seven, thus ending a 14-year drought during which she had no US hits at all. At the time of writing, in January 2005, her new two-disc greatest hits album, *Ultimate Kylie*, had not yet been released in the United States (but had been available elsewhere in the world since November 15, 2004), whereas Britney Spears's 2004 release, *Greatest Hits: My Prerogative*, had already spent nine weeks in the *Billboard* albums chart and peaked at number four.

"It's easier to break into America from inside of America," speculated Philadelphia native Jamie Klingler, the international licensing manager at the photo agency Corbis Outline in London. The company provides photos, many from the lens of the best celebrity photographers in the world, to British periodicals like *FHM, Hello!* and *OK!*, which deal exclusively in celebrity material.

All the A-list stars have had their glossy selves pass through Klingler's filter. "Kylie didn't become a sex symbol for like six or seven years into her career," Klingler pointed out. "And even then, she has never taken it to the extremes that Britney has. Whereas Britney stopped being known for her music early, early on. She really played the media much better than I think Kylie has, especially the American media. The whole, 'Oh, I'm a virgin, I'm a virgin, I'm a virgin' but 'I'm a Slave 4 U' – the dichotomy between the two made her a 'virgin whore' and really played that up, to the kids and to the fathers, to all of that."

"I think a lot has changed because of money," she mused. "And because of the 'sex sells' thing. Now, you can't really be a sexy Britney Spears type of person without doing *FHM*. Like Mary-Kate and Ashley Olsen, there was a whole thing about them turning 18 and the countdown to them being legal. And there's the Paris Hilton porn thing. It's almost like our culture has allowed pedophilia, to a certain extent, to become sexy and cool. It's expected and almost laughed about that men should lust after these 16 and 17 year-old girls.

"I'm not saying that it's a 'victim' culture for young women that are playing the game, but Britney doing 'Hit me baby one more time' because she's a sexy schoolgirl? She wasn't trying to look like it was hip-hop and bubblegum, she was trying to look like Lolita. The Lolita thing was a literary thing, but now it's in your face all the time."

A certain tawdry sensibility, she added, has crept into idol worship today; the words "glamour" and "celebrity" held a much different meaning in the past.

"I think of the movie stars of the 1930s and the 1940s, and how some stars now have totally trashed that. However they might have had fake marriages and fake relationships, at least there was a gloss and a glamour and you felt like there was an air around it. Whereas now, it's not like there's any air of beauty or grace around Britney's newest marriage."

In her zone

So what can one safely surmise then, about the star power of Britney Spears? In her most recent *In The Zone* DVD, fans received an "intimate" look at her backstage time, sharing time with family and friends (introducing her mother and grandfather as well as her kid sister, a blonde nymphet herself). In all her dance routines, Britney walked the thin line between the blatant and the suggestive, with a confident sassiness that keeps the viewer enthralled, long enough to resist questioning deeper motives. Perhaps her real talent is not unlike that of Madonna's, to serve as a modern-day *agent provocateur*, to push the buttons and shove the envelope, past all those dark places in your mind that most people dare not go. All the while neatly packaged, as a sugary, teen-dream idol.

Britney's iconic images project a knowing victory, of the kind that says that America has succeeded in colonizing the minds of young people the world over, because such images are what they want to see. A smiling, Stepford wife-in-training gyrating to bump-and-grind moves is infinitely more appealing to the eye of a teenager than some anorexic-thin can-can dancer, even if she possesses a derrière to die for. Kylie Minogue, conversely, appeals to an older, more mature audience, whose numbers will never be as big as Britney's core audience. Britney's career is also fascinating in terms of how one person's status has bloomed from mere idol to world icon.

She flew out of the gate as simply the latest in a line of would-be teen queens, but broke away from the pack simply because there were multiple dimensions to her persona that people could tap into for their own purposes.

A long article devoted to this very topic, in the *New York Times* in March 2004, made note of the proliferation of Britney Spears websites on the Internet. There are "dress like Britney" sites devoted to her fashion sensibility, and even animated, faux-documentary sites like the one from *LiquidGeneration.com* called "Mystery of Britney's Spears' Breasts," which chronicles the "varying appearances of the star's bosom."

The piece also made note of how Britney's public appearances can evoke spectacular changes in the marketing of products. Two instances were cited: first, Britney accidentally spilled the contents of her purse before boarding a place at London's Heathrow Airport and the paparazzi zoomed in on a bottle of Zantrex-3, a popular diet pill, among its contents. A few months later, the American paparazzi snapped her leaving a bookstore with the book *Listening to Prozac*. Sales for both the pills and the book accordingly went up (Basic Research, the pill's manufacturer, confirmed this), and the article reiterated a commonly held belief that "photos like these humanize the pop star and allow Average Janes to feel okay about their battles with depression, obesity and other issues."

However, the *New York Times* also interviewed experts like Tricia Rose, professor of American Studies at University of California Santa Cruz, who issued this riposte: "I am very cynical about these kinds of things. There's such a media engine behind all these superstars, and now they can't survive without it. Why is it that if Britney wanted a book about Prozac, why wouldn't she just order it on Amazon? She knows the cameras are on her 24/7."

Of course, she does. She has, after all, allowed herself to be seen publicly smoking and drinking, since they're typically symptomatic of teen rebellion. (Lots of teenagers can identify with her!) Of the infamous mouth-to-mouth kiss with Madonna at the 2003 MTV Video Music awards, Britney mugs the camera in her *In The Zone* DVD, holding up the cover of *Us* magazine featuring the two of them. And, giggling, she lip-synchs the big, bold headline: "We're hot new best friends!"

If ever there was an admission that she knows how her bread is buttered, that was certainly it. The ditzy blonde chick persona is a perfect foil. Contracted to Pepsi (as a spokesperson of the "Pepsi generation"), she allowed herself to be photographed walking down a street wearing a T-shirt emblazoned with a mock-Pepsi logo that read: "Sexsi." Major magazines like *Us* always require photo approval from her, via her publicist, especially for a cover with a headline screaming, "Britney Out of Control," followed by the subhead, "New shocking wedding details. All-night partying. Public tears. Why pop's former good girl is suddenly so bad."

Suddenly so bad? The transition is hardly sudden, and is very much calculated. "She has reached major icon status on a worldwide level," observed Matthew Donahue, professor of popular culture at Bowling Green State University. "She still appeals to young girls and she now appeals to young women. It's the best crossover you could ask for."

How can Kylie Minogue compete with that? Britney had already cast the merchandising net much wider, having endorsed a range of products from Clairol shampoo to Skechers shoes, when the Australian press started writing worshipfully about the Love Kylie lingerie line (Kylie was seen modeling them herself in the May 2003 issue of Australian *Vogue*; notably the Love Kylie Dolly bra (A$50) and matching full brief (A$23), Love Kylie black mesh Diva underwire bra (A$40), Love Kylie black mesh Diva hipster briefs with suspenders (A$23). Kylie's major problem, though, might simply be one of timing – Britney and her fans had come of age in the Internet era, where things happened at lightning speed and achievement no longer occurred exponentially.

At the time of writing, the latest Britney news involved sales of her chewing gum on the online auction site *eBay* – two dozen vendors, all claiming their rubbery wads had been spat out by Britney herself, reported by the Associated Press. The top price was US$14,000, though most others were significantly less. Some were selling her crushed cigarette butts, too.

One in London asked US$53 for a piece of gum, supposedly obtained at her 2000 Wembley Arena concert. A Canadian seller asked US$1,000 and claimed it would pass a DNA test. Yet another offered for sale a piece of gum which "still has her teeth marks on it," taken from the 2004 MTV Video Music awards. Dental records need not be verified, however, since it was clearly a fake, because Britney did not attend the event that night. Still, can one blame the poor guy for trying?

Jamie Klingler

Jamie Klingler is the international licensing manager at the London office of the photo agency Corbis Outline. The Philadelphia native formerly worked in New York, where she dealt with celebrities through their publicists, working "clearances" for "photo approval," the process by which magazines buy celebrity photos for publication.

Where is the overlap between you and the publicists in terms of creating celebrity branding?

We work in conjunction. Our goal is the sale. It isn't to promote their image or to help them get a bigger name. Our goal is to get as much money as possible for it. Part of it is to create the need for it, to play the magazines off each other for the best stuff. The publicist will want his or her client's picture in the best quality magazines, whereas we want the picture in the magazine that will pay us the most money.

But they dictate the media outlet, don't they?

Yes, they totally do. They can say yes or no. We don't have the power. They can veto us.

Celebrity photography has become much more competitive now, hasn't it, in terms of how "celebrity news" is "created"?

Yes. I think in the UK, it's even more manufactured than it is in the US, with magazines like *OK!* and *Hello!*, where the magazine will pay for their trip and then, 'Oh my God, a photographer caught them making out in a pool!' It's all so staged. And almost accepted, that it is so. I think the US is actually starting to follow the UK in terms of all the celebrity rags, with more picture-based stuff. The amount of money they'll pay for a J. Lo picture when J. Lo was at the height, where we had these pictures of J. Lo in her little pink knickers, they paid huge, huge money. Because their circulation would go through the roof.

We live in an oversaturated celebrity-media world now. Why do you think this has happened?

I think a lot has changed because of money. And because of the "sex sells" thing. Like Mary-Kate and Ashley Olsen, there was a whole thing about them turning 18 and the countdown to them being legal. And there's the Paris Hilton porn thing. It's almost like our culture has allowed pedophilia, to a certain extent, to become sexy and cool. The other part of it is the ADD culture – the attention-deficit disorder. We have now got a five-minute attention span to remember who the celebrities are!

The feeding frenzy would not exist in part without you, though, don't you agree?

Right. And they're hungrier and hungrier for it. It's a question that always comes up. The fact is that I am trying to sell the sexiest pictures I can find of

Lindsay Lohan, and the biggest amount of money I get for any supplement is the "*FHM* 100 Sexiest." I bring in a lot of money for my photographers. A lot of people shoot the *FHM* stuff so they can shoot their own work. It allows them to live their lifestyle. So, are we creating the celebrity frenzy or are we feeding it? Or is it chicken and eggs?

But do you have a problem with this, in terms of personal culpability, since you help to create the need for sexual imagery?

My problem with my job is more often one where sessions with half-naked girls come in and it means money for me. I was a Film and Women's Studies major, so there's my feminist pedagogy! But if I see a picture where she's half-naked, I know I'm going to get money. I know I'm going to hit my goals, I know I'll make commission, so I'm going to sell it as much as I can. I made a ton of money off J. Lo's ass!

8
Between Credibility and Caricature: The Zen of Being Tom Cruise and Brad Pitt

"Difficult? This is *Mission: Impossible*. Difficult should be a walk in the park for you." So uttered Anthony Hopkins to Tom Cruise, in John Woo's film *Mission: Impossible 2*. How then, to consider the start-stop production of its sequel *Mission: Impossible 3*? One month before the beginning of principal photography, in July 2003, director Joe Carnahan had walked off the project, citing "creative differences." The previous choice, David Fincher, had already left, ostensibly to helm another project, while a slew of writers had already come and gone. The film's star and producer then began hunting for a new director himself ("reviewing a list of about half a dozen candidates," reported the wire service Agence France-Presse).

The star and producer is, of course, Tom Cruise.

The film, of course, will somehow get made. Paramount Pictures will ensure that it delivers another installment of a successful franchise. The first *Mission: Impossible*, directed by Brian de Palma in 1996, grossed US$454 million worldwide. The sequel, directed by John Woo in 2000, grossed US$546 million. So, now saddled with a production budget of some $150 million, how could they afford to fail?

Hollywood movies used to be driven by studio bosses, but now they're driven by stars. Big stars, as they say, can "open" movies by inducing people to pay for theatre tickets, seduced by the strength of their famous names.

Branding is, of course, about seduction. "How do you build a new brand? With public relations, not advertising," noted marketing guru Al Ries. And there is no better form of public relations for a movie than the pulling power of a star who is an A-list Hollywood celebrity. This art of managing "mindshare" is a deft balancing act, requiring the cooperation of many elements: the star, the star's publicist, and on a supporting-cast level the star's managers, agents, and lawyers.

However, all would be sound and fury signifying nothing were it not for the star himself. Why else would Tom Cruise turn on his charm and flash that killer smile for the cameras? Women swoon at the sight, while some men might grimace enviously at just how well he does it. "Cruise, who's handsome the way sports cars are," observed cultural critic Tom Carson in the July 2002 issue of *Esquire*, is "walking proof of the difference between being a actor and being a movie star.... Cruise is the kind of performer whose art is most interesting when understood as a metaphor for his career trajectory."

Elevator shoes

And what a trajectory it has been. Thomas Cruise Mapother IV leapt from obscurity in 1983, with a Golden Globe nomination for *Risky Business*, a mere two years after his film debut in *Taps*, but it wasn't until 1986 when the larger world heard his name – thanks to a monster hit about fighter pilots called *Top Gun*.

The rest is history: Three Golden Globes (for *Born on the Fourth of July, Jerry Maguire*, and *Magnolia*; Cruise was nominated for Oscars for all three but did not win), and a list of memorable performances (*Rain Man, The Color of Money, Far and Away, Days of Thunder, The Firm, Interview with the Vampire, Vanilla Sky*, and the *Mission: Impossible* series). Many of these demonstrate how someone with Cruise's good looks can walk that thin line between credibility and caricature.

One of the stronger elements of his craft is the fact that his acting is often so good that it forces the viewer to look past those chiseled cheekbones and the disarming smile. His personal charm is linked to his choice of film roles, in much the same way that say Rock Hudson was, in the 1950s and 1960s. Cruise is a major box-office draw even when the movie finds him in an unsympathetic role (like the sexist cad in *Magnolia*) or when the movie itself receives mixed notices (Tom Carson has noted, "Demonstrations of star power don't come much starker than Cruise single-handedly prodding a muddled stinker like *Vanilla Sky* past the US$100 million mark.")

What his adoring public doesn't see, of course, is the sheer effort taken to maintain his star power.

Things are arranged to accommodate him. For the 1995 film *Interview with the Vampire*, Cruise was apparently given special elevator shoes to wear, so that he could look taller in his scenes with co-star Brad Pitt. Everyone remembers the way Cruise went head-to-head with Jack Nicholson in *A Few Good Men*, acquitting himself

166

decently despite confronting a star of his own stature, but that was an exception to the norm – in most of his films, directors ensure that the supporting cast has to be exceptionally good, simply because Cruise is always the centre of attention.

In interviews when he is asked to talk about his technique, Cruise likes to say he is big on visualizing the scene; in his own terminology he needs to "restimulate" (as he told James Lipton and an *Inside the Actor's Studio* audience), hoping of course that the audience will empathize with his projection. Why else did so many people go to see *The Last Samurai*, even if they've never seen *The Seven Samurai* (or any of Kurosawa epics), let alone had any personal interest in medieval Japan?

The film was a moderate success, but it would have truly died a *seppuku* death had Cruise's co-star, the veteran Japanese actor Ken Watanabe, not turned in his quietly magnificent performance (which earned him an Oscar nomination), though this is neatly balanced by Cruise being depicted as a man of integrity and valour, the very qualities his fans wanted to see. Cruise is the very epitome of what Hollywood's starmaking machinery does so well, the art of packaging an idol for mass consumption.

When Cruise filed for divorce from Nicole Kidman in 2001, his then-publicist Pat Kingsley announced the end of the ten-year marriage as due to "difficulties inherent in divergent careers" – questionably suspicious, since the couple worked together frequently and seldom spent more than two weeks apart. Cruise's ex-wife Mimi Rogers, however, was somewhat less diplomatic; she gave an interview that summer to the *Daily Telegraph* in London, which was summarily picked up by gossip columnist Liz Smith, who then quoted Rogers in the *Los Angeles Times* on July 6, 2001.

"It looked as though marriage wouldn't fit into his overall spiritual need," Rogers recalled. At one stage in their marriage, Rogers perhaps incautiously revealed, Cruise was seriously thinking of becoming a monk. "He thought he had to be celibate to maintain the purity of his instrument. *My* instrument needed tuning."

Ouch. And it begs some questions: What is it about the human condition that makes movie stars so attractive as archetypes, to the point where some need to be knocked off their pedestals? Why is the press famous for building up and tearing down the stars they help create? And why don't the Pat Kingsleys of the world see that for all the prevarication and euphemism they so masterfully conjure, a whole generation of moviegoers who subscribe to *Premiere* have now wised up to filmstar divorces and "divergent careers."

Nevertheless, the press and publicity machines have conspired successfully to rehash archetype ideals, so as to perpetuate the mythology of the pop culture icon. The key issue here is the process by which the transition takes place – from idol to icon.

Leather miniskirt

Brad Pitt is perhaps the best case in point. Who remembers the first time they saw him? Most fans will cite the Ridley Scott film *Thelma and Louise*, in which he played the seductive hitchhiker, the "mysterious stranger" who embodied sexual frisson – the kind that turns heads in darkened movie theatres and makes them wonder, 'Wow, who the hell is that actor?!!!" He reinstated this theme with several offbeat, edgy roles – the serial killer (*Kalifornia*), the vampire (*Interview with the Vampire*), the asylum inmate (*12 Monkeys*, for which he won a Golden Globe and secured his first Oscar nomination). Some fans even remember films in which his accent could barely be understood (*Snatch, The Devil's Own*), and character-driven films where he was cast somewhat against type (*A River Runs Through It, Seven Years in Tibet*).

But no matter. It was his second Golden Globe nomination, however, that made him a idol to female audiences, when he played the freespirited wanderer Tristan in *Legends of the Fall*. And then there was the doomed Martin Brest film *Meet Joe Black* (which lit him gorgeously, offsetting the meandering storyline) and the cult favorite *Fight Club* (which did not light him favorably, but had a superb storyline) and, finally, a historical epic of ancient Greece called *Troy* ("a gilded Brad Pitt with a leather miniskirt and a Heathrow duty-free accent," noted the delightfully irreverent *New*

York Times pundit Maureen Dowd) which opened in the United States on May 14, 2004 with a US$45 million box-office weekend.

Troy's success was sheer proof of Pitt's power, surely, since co-stars Orlando Bloom and Eric Bana can hardly claim credit for so many ticket sales, especially among young women willing to sit through a war epic. (Bloom's fans may disagree, though it is my understanding that his fans are mostly teenage girls and Pitt's female audience skews slightly older.) There are things in it, the astute critic A. O. Scott noted, "that remind you why you like movies in the first place." It is essentially the same old story told anew – good versus evil, with a hero to cheer for, and a narrative that can traipse the action tightrope without condescending to its audience. (One need only imagine, say, Jean-Claude Van Damme or Steven Seagal in the same role to visualize and understand the difference.)

The curiously triumphant thing about *Troy* is that Pitt, as the warrior Achilles, manages to make his character work despite the over-the-top earnestness of a historical epic that takes vast liberties with history, condensing a ten-year war into a two-week time frame, told in two hours of screen time. "Pitt attacks the role with the same vigor and agility the character demonstrates in combat," Scott noted. "Achilles' narcissism is like that of a modern celebrity: he fights because it will bring him fame, not to serve the gods or the glory of the Greek nation or, least of all, his corrupt king. His true loyalty is to individuals .... rather than to causes."

That's precisely the thing that Johnny Depp meant when, in many past interviews, he said that he "doesn't do the Tom Cruise thing." (Meaning, movies where he gets paid US$4 million are fine by him; he doesn't need a Cruise-size US$20 million-per-movie salary.) What he also means it that being a true celebrity also means behaving true to oneself, a firmness that paid off handsomely for him when his own swashbuckling role (in *Pirates of the Caribbean: The Curse of the Black Pearl*) earned him a Golden Globe Best Actor award and enough rave notices to get him hired for the sequel (for much more than US$4 million, of course).

Like Pitt, Depp has nurtured his celebrity much more carefully than some would suspect, and his marriage to French actress/singer Vanessa

169

Paradis actually boosted his mystique and heightened mass-audience curiosity. There is point to this: Movie fans usually read a ton of movie press, most of which is filtered through a prism fueled by publicity and marketing. Stars have a complicity in this process, and they owe their success to the way they manipulate this to their advantage.

Take, for instance, all the early interviews that Brad Pitt did before fame took over his life. In May 1989, he told photojournalist Karen Hardy Bystedt about how he got his foot in the door by attaining what every aspiring actor needs: an agent. Within three months of moving to Los Angeles from his native Missouri, he got into a good acting class, which led to him being "discovered" by agents.

"I was driving strippers around on weekends to make extra money at night," he recalls. "I'd take them to bachelor parties. I did it for about two months and then I couldn't hang with it. But then, on the last night I drove, one of the new strippers told me about this acting class. A famous actor friend of hers, whose name I won't mention, went to this class. So, I figured, if that person's in it, it's good enough for me. I went to it. It was great. Then I got a scene partner. She had an audition with the Triad agency. She asked me if I'd do the scene we prepared for class in front of all these agents. I said, 'Yeah, I guess so, whatever.' Boom, I got signed.

"It was a scene from *Ordinary People*. No, she didn't get signed. The fact was they took a gamble on me because I'd never done anything and I wasn't in the union. But then, that's half the battle."

Bystedt used that quote in her chapter on Pitt in her 1996 book *Before They Were Famous* (which also featured the early years of Keanu Reeves, Willem Dafoe, Johnny Depp, John Cusack, Christian Slater, Courtney Cox, Sandra Bullock, and others, told in their own words). The pivotal element in Pitt's story was that he was inspired by someone else's celebrity, which led to the acting class which, in turn, sent him on the way to his own fame.

The agent who signed him, Bill Danzinger from the Triad agency, believed enough in him to get him parts that few today even know about. His first roles were on television: *Dallas, Growing Pains, 21 Jump Street*. His first two feature films followed – "A movie that hopefully will never be out called *Cutting Class*," as he himself admitted (It has since been released on DVD; a teenage, high-school horror flick strictly for the hardcore Pitt fans) and then *Dark Side of the Sun*, a coming-of-age teen drama shot in Yugoslavia. And then a pilot for another television series, *The Kids Are Alright*, shot in Canada. At the time, Pitt was living in reduced circumstances, with a roommate who kept borrowing his underwear ("I'm doing the old reversal boxer routine.... God forbid if we ran out of toilet paper.") in a house without a television ("It broke down three months ago").

Interior design

Those were events he surely laughs about now. It matters little too that almost nobody remembers any of those early films. Struggling along like a normal nobody has turned into the stuff of legend. It becomes romantic now because a star's pre-celebrity period meant enduring sundry indignities, which people buy into for metaphysical reasons: because, deep down, they too yearn for similar deliverance, in their own lives. Celebrity gossip magazines like *People* in the United States, *Hello!* in the United Kingdom and *New Idea* in Australia all exist to perpetuate such mythologies.

The *National Enquirer* and *News of the World*, and other such saucy publications, even pay sources for stories, and have been known to assign reporters to do bizarre things - like ferret through a celebrity's trash to literally dig out the dirt. Prescription drugs are always fair game (a pitfall of celebrityhood is the careful disposal of Tylenol and Xanax bottles, as well as condoms and suppositories). All manner of apocrypha and maledicta can emerge from hither and yon ("Uma Thurman threw used condoms out of her hotel room window, I saw her do it myself!" one film crew member exclaimed, refusing of course to be identified by name), making for water-cooler gossip writ large.

In such light, stories about the home Brad Pitt shared with Jennifer Aniston in the Hollywood Hills always made a point about the interior design (theirs was in the French-Normandy style, with leather Eames chairs in the living room), and some came neatly sun-dappled with handy quotes from Pitt himself about his domestic life ("Neither of us wants to be the spokesman for happy marriage, for couple-dom"). Of course, this was before the infamous Pitt–Aniston split-up of January 2005, which led the American celebrity magazine *Us Weekly* to achieve its highest-selling issue ever ("How Jen found out," the issue of February 7, 2005, which sold 1.25 million copies). The magazine also rushed to press a book, *Brad & Jen: The rise and fall of Hollywood's golden couple*, hitting bookstores the week of February 21.

Publishing a book to quickly capitalize on someone's misfortune might seem tasteless, but to be fair the said "golden couple" had drawn sincere admiration from many cultural observers who saw symbolic value in them as a duo, and who were now probably chagrined at their dissolution. "Brad Pitt and Jennifer Aniston, as a couple, I'd say, are icons," declared Jamie Klingler, the international licensing manager at the London office of the celebrity photo agency Corbis Outline. "Because they increase each other's star power instead of decrease each other's star power." (Klingler was interviewed for this book before the break-up.)

One wonders how many people have attempted to quit smoking because of what they read about Pitt preparing for the role of Achilles in *Troy*? "I quit smoking – and let me tell you, I was a professional smoker and I still miss it," he told *Vanity Fair*. "I know she was trying to kill me but I really loved the bitch." And then, in the summer of 2004, stories circulated that the Pitts were going to adopt a baby after four years of trying ("I think it's time, I think we have been in rehearsals long enough," Pitt had cheekily quipped a few months prior), sending the tabloids a-tizzy again. They were seen shopping for a country house in Sussex (to raise a child in England à la Madonna, some speculated).

Perhaps there's nothing like impending childbirth to rekindle interest in celebrities, especially since Pitt's ex-girlfriend Gwyneth Paltrow had already given birth. (People want them to succeed, since the propagation of the human species is at stake, for goodness sake!)

"The thing about our marriage is that there was an opening in the Hollywood couple slot and, unfortunately, we've fallen into it," Pitt casually said at the end of 2001. He was 35 then, and Aniston 32. "We are treated as special. We get away with things that other people can't. And you start to believe the lie that you are special, that you're better than other people. You start demanding that kind of treatment." In a profession where the bottom line requires actors to deliver word-perfect lines from a written script, it is highly ironic that fame is often a matter of following the script.

There was a time when Hollywood agents didn't specify that their client would be "attached" to a project if and only if they could be assured "above-the-title credit." But times have changed. Filming budgets, once considered high at US$20 million, now seem puny at US$100 million, and so a big-star client being "attached" to a project implies a surefire guarantee of the necessary investor money. It's all a game, and stardom can depend on how well one plays.

Because nothing is ever a surefire thing, and even once-willing participants can become detractors. Singer/songwriter Maria McKee, for instance, once told me that she wasn't all that thrilled about the way her song, "Show Me Heaven" was used as the "Love Theme" for the 1990 Tom Cruise film *Days of Thunder*, even though the song became her biggest hit even as the film itself well and truly bombed. "I did find the whole experience somewhat unsettling and embarrassing – Tom Cruise and Nicole Kidman sucking face and then, all of a sudden, I'm edited in," she blanched. "That's just a little bit on the weird side for me. Not exactly my original vision."

Yet we all cling to the vision, because its gatekeepers insist on its authenticity. We want to believe in Tom and Nicole, or Tom and Penelope, or Brad and Gwyneth, or Brad and Jennifer. Or, in actuality, in what their publicists say. "Being real is good," the late Stanley Kubrick once said, in reference to Cruise and Kidman in his last film, *Eyes Wide Shut*, "but being interesting is better."

Hans Ebert

Hans Ebert is Executive Director of EMI Music Southeast Asia, and he was formerly Marketing Director of Universal Music, both in Hong Kong. Prior to becoming a record company executive, he was an advertising agency creative director and also a correspondent for the music industry trade journal, *Billboard*.

Legend has it that you "discovered" Maggie Cheung when you were an advertising agency creative director. Is that true?

Yes. I used Maggie in the first-ever commercial she ever did for McDonald's. She was 17 and she was in Hong Kong from London. This was 1978. I paid her HK$300 and she worked two days. The commercial won a Clio award in New York.

What did you see in her and how did that happen?

I just knew right away, that this girl was going to be a star. The fact that she is now considered "the Catherine Deneuve of Asia," I'm not really surprised. I was with DDB Needham at the time. Production houses always come and give you videotapes with 12 or 15 girls, and Maggie was one of the girls. She had not been in anything at the time. Nothing. She was very cute, she had this really cute

Cockney accent. That commercial for McDonald's had to do with being able to dance and she had a sense of rhythm, and she photographed well, which was good – because she had three other commercials to do! She worked on four McDonald's commercials in Hong Kong, all in one month.

What is your view of the impact of Asia on the West, in terms of celebrities and popular culture?

It started with Bruce Lee. He is an icon with black Americans, and rappers today still identify with Bruce. Because he was the underdog, and rappers see themselves as underdogs. But there is a huge difference between the film industry and the music industry. How do we make our artists as hip as a Wong Kar-wai or as a Bruce Lee? We don't have a musical equivalent or an Asian musical answer to Bruce Lee. I've been wracking my brain about this. Why have Chinese film directors and even cinematographers been embraced by Hollywood, whereas we have made zero impression with our music? It is strange. I think it is a racial thing. And there's this thing called "martial arts" and "kung-fu."

Why do you think there is so much emphasis on music celebrity now, even in the mainstream, non-music media?

Because the worlds of music and advertising have criss-crossed. I think this is still the tip of the iceberg. Ad agencies have always been suspicious of music companies. They've always thought we're just trying to flog them a bunch of goods. Music companies think ad agency guys are poseurs. But the day has now come, when they're both saying, "Look guys, we better get together, because we're after the same consumer's dollar. So why don't we work together instead of competing?" So we're now forming alliances with ad agencies.

How does this work, internally, between a company like yours and a company wanting a consumer product endorsement?

It's really up to the advertiser and the marketing director, though sometimes I wonder about the marketing directors today. How much do they know about music? How much do they know about consumers? And how much do they actually pay to get to know the consumer? Without knowing the consumer, you can't really do it. I've had a lot of advertisers make very subjective decisions.

What happens in such a situation?

Sometimes I actually try to talk them out of it, because it could actually hurt the act. You can pay a lot of money, but you can kill the act's career by being associated with a bum brand, one that does not complement the image of the act. You can take all that money but, from a long-term point of view, it can cripple your career. For us, at EMI, we pride ourselves in building long-lasting careers. I don't want to get involved with "pop idol" kind of shows. Those are here today, gone tomorrow.

What do you think of William Hung?

William Hung, I think, is a disgrace to Asians. Because what was a joke has now become, I think, an insult. It just plays to American audiences who think that Asians have buck teeth and can't dance and are bad lovers. I think actually the worst part is that his parents are part of this. I think that's really, really sad. They're typical Hong Kong. They've made this kid of theirs into a cartoon character and they want people to pay for this. The joke's gone, the punch line is dead. I feel sorry for William Hung, but I'm pissed off at his parents.

9
Double Trouble: The Silhouette Stardom of Shelley Michelle

Like every aspiring actress in Hollywood, Shelley Michelle daydreamed of her career lynchpin, the role that would fulfill her destiny and catapult her to stardom. And why not? She was young, pretty, and blonde, and she had no problems taking her clothes off.

Luckily for her, the last part of that equation made it all happen. She had no inkling of the future on the fateful day she came in as a "body double" for the lead actress, a lass from Smyrna, Georgia who was then five films into her career and shooting for success herself. The movie starred Richard Gere and it was directed by Garry Marshall. Something called *Pretty Woman*. And the actress's name was Julia Roberts.

"After I did *Pretty Woman*, it just snowballed for me," Michelle recalled. "It was such a huge movie. After that, every star, if they needed a body double, they called me. I definitely became the most famous body double in the world, and I feel having this claim to fame is a mark in history that no one else has."

She had, you could say, no time for false humility. Indeed, she had almost no time at all. In 12 years, she'd doubled for more than 100 stars, most notably Sandra Bullock, Barbra Streisand, Kim Basinger, and Madonna. Her website is none other than *www.bodydouble.com*, and her own talent agency, Body Doubles & Parts, Inc., teaches aspiring young starlets her style of imparting illusion.

Her calling card is herself, a walking epitome of "personal branding" with a wicked twist. For what better illusion can there be in celebrity culture than one where the viewer is fooled into eyeing an actress onscreen, especially when watching her disrobe, only to learn later than it was actually someone else? Her work could almost exist as the definitive send-up of the idea of movie star as cultural icon.

"I call it 'kinaesthetic acting,' because I have to mimic them," she explained. "I have to watch the actress to see how she moves, in order to make it believable, that it is in fact the actress's body. I have to do all these things, like she has to be scared or happy or passive or sad. I have to put that through my body."

Being naked on-camera was always part of the job, since body doubles often stand in for stars armed with that irksome "no nudity" clause in their contracts. "Well, some stars don't like doing that on a set where you have all the crew looking," Michelle noted. "I think it's an honor to work with all these stars, you're right there with these A-list actors, and you get to work with the best directors, you learn camera angles. It's a really great way to break into the business. I mean, hey, I was personally chosen by Sandra Bullock! I was approved by her to shoot the box cover for the DVD release, too. The film was *A Fool and His Money*. They said she's very straight up and down in the body and they wanted to give her some curves!"

The naked truth

Shelley Michelle was born in Hollywood, California, on April 3, 1968, of mixed European descent ("German, Irish, Swedish, and a drop of French"). Prior to acting, she had taught in a modeling school and also taught ballet. (She's studied with the Joffrey Ballet in New York and had been a Ford model.) Fresh out of high school, she sang and danced in the band Kid Creole and the Coconuts. "My mother was a model and a ballet dancer so she put me in the same from the age of three, and I took to the dancing and modeling like a duck to water."

She graduated from the University of Southern California, received an Outstanding Student acting scholarship and went on to study in Edinburgh, Scotland, where she performed in 15 plays, six of them lead roles.

Her own agency began after she'd invited the Screen Actors Guild (the Hollywood film actors' union) to visit her sets to see what she was doing. "They had no idea there were body doubles! I teach aspiring body doubles in my agency how to move, how to be fluid with their bodies, keep their head high and out of the way of the camera. After *Pretty Woman*, the guild wrote body doubles into its by-laws. And that's why I started my agency. Because of my agency, we now get credited the same as actresses."

"I'm proud to have made a positive change in the industry," she declared. "I didn't receive credit for *Pretty Woman* but I believe

Pretty Woman made me very famous in my niche. My favorite celebrity to double is still Julia Roberts in that movie. She kept thanking me personally and she was so humble at the time since it was her first big movie, too."

To think that it all started with her legs, which have since been insured by Lloyds of London for US$1 million. The film was *My Stepmother is an Alien*, a vehicle for Kim Basinger. An actress was required to "double" for her legs.

Michelle remembered being selected from 5,000 pairs of legs at 20th Century-Fox. That was her first "part," the humble start for a nascent career. She has since been featured in some 300 newspapers and magazines (*People*, with the headline "Double Indemnity"; *In Style*, in its "Hottest Bodies" issue; *Allure*, under "The Naked Truth"), and has also appeared on television (CNN, *Entertainment Tonight, E! News Live*, and, of course, *Howard Stern*).

As fate would have it, it was an article about her in the *Los Angeles Times* that led director Phil Joannou to call her for a part in his film *Final Analysis*, in which she would "body double" for – Kim Basinger. A vicious cycle, it might be deemed, almost literally – they wanted more than just her legs this time, and Basinger had something to say about it.

"Phil Joannou called me in and he put me in a trailer and she was being unruly about that," Michelle recalled. Basinger had, of course, appeared in *Playboy* and erotic films like *Nine and a Half Weeks*, so she clearly had no qualms about doing her own nudity. "Kim actually did not want a body double. She did not want her body to look like she had some work done, like a breast job or something, but the director insisted on one."

"I ended up opening the whole movie with my body parts, which you think is Kim Basinger. I'm wearing lingerie and it looks like I'm undressing and that runs over the opening titles of the film."

"There was another scene, which got cut," she added. "Eric Roberts is saying, 'Take your clothes off!' and Kim's looking very nervous. She didn't want to do that scene. It scared her. So that scene was shot with me. But they ended up cutting it. It was the best part, and they didn't use it!"

Her most memorable "audition" was for Catherine Oxenberg, the *Dynasty* star, who was looking for a body double to play her in a 1990 film ironically called *Overexposed*. "It was down to the top six girls and she wanted to see everybody in person," Michelle recalled. "It was against her morals to appear nude because she's a Yugoslavian princess. So she went through 150 girls and it came down to six of us. She said to me, 'You look Swedish, you look just like me. But do you mind taking your top off?'

"And I said, 'Sure,' and took my top off right in front of her. I think she was way more embarrassed than I was! She just said, 'Oh, you're perfect, that'll work!' That was a strange one. I think that was the only one where that happened, where you're actually stripping in front of the star. You don't normally do that. Usually, the director will shoot your body and show it to the star and say, 'What do you think?'"

Unavailable for dinner

Sometimes the star doesn't appear, having granted approval for a body double. This happened when Michelle doubled for Barbra Streisand. "It was on *The Prince of Tides*, for a shot of her legs on the couch. They wanted her legs to be in a shorter skirt and look very sexy. They actually brought me the exact suit she wore and let me keep it after the shoot."

Body doubling is a inexact science, no matter how similar the resemblance, because it is a rarefied art of sorts – rendering perfectly the look and feel of something you're not actually doing. Like when you appear to be having sex, in something that's not a porno film. "There's a lot more to body doubling than meets the eye," Michelle emphasized. "If I do a love scene, it's very mechanical. I doubled for Anne Archer and did this love scene with Dennis Hopper. It was a cable movie, called *Nails*."

"He picks her up and he puts her on the bed and he started kissing her, and boom! They cut to the body double," she recalled. "It was my body on top of him. And we rolled and he's on top of me.

When I was lying on top of him, they said I gave her like ten years to her career because I made her body look so good."

Yes, but how did Dennis Hopper's react?

"Dennis Hopper, that was like the scariest one I've ever done," she laughed. "Because he really wanted it to 'look real.' So he tried to make the sex look real."

Like he wanted to really have sex with her? "Yes, I think so!" she squealed. "But the thing is, in body doubling, I think, if it feels good it doesn't look good to the camera. Because body doubling is more mechanical. My face has to be out of it, my head's up, and I'm using my body. I'm thinking of camera angles, and you can't just go for it.

"So that's what I say: if it feels good, it probably doesn't look good. You're always thinking of the angles and what's going to look good with your body in it, your legs have to placed strategically and stuff like that. It's far more complicated and more than meets the eye. Anyway, Dennis, he was just goin' for it! He followed me to my trailer afterwards. He wanted to scene to go on and I'm like, 'No no no, I'm just the body double!'"

"A lot of the actors will be mistaken about my job," she sighed. "Because I come in and do a love scene, and make this actress's body look great, doesn't mean that I'm available for dinner afterwards!"

Hollywood has always had its issues with nudity, and sometimes events transpire to prove a point about sexual objectification: There's no nude like a famous nude. In her autobiography, *My Story*, Marilyn Monroe recalled the now-famous nude calendar she shot with photographer Tom Kelley. She was then still a struggling actress, fighting to get her car back after it had been repossessed for non-payment of monthly installments.

The young Norma Dougherty needed the money, and Kelley needed some nudes for a calendar. "You're ideal for the job not only because you have a fine shape but you're unknown," Kelley told her. "Nobody'll recognize you. It'll just be a picture of a beautiful nobody." Shortly later, of course, she became a beautiful somebody. A contract with 20th Century-Fox and a change of name changed all that. (Marilyn was suggested by the studio boss, Monroe was her mother's maiden name.) Nobody can remember her first film, *Scudda Hoo, Scudda Hey*, because all her parts were cut.

But did it matter? In December 1953, Hugh Hefner made a mint, and then some, from Tom Kelley's calendar photo, when he used it to launch his magazine called *Playboy*. The creation of an icon is always best viewed in hindsight, because one gets the perspective in full. Artifice is wielded, legends are concocted, and a "nobody" became a "somebody."

There were three ways, Monroe had posited in her autobiography, by which one became a famous movie star. The first was through a single spellbinding performance in a particular film. The second was when the studio saw a "star possibility" and got its publicity machine to flood the press with wild stories about the new star's "wonderful character and fascinating oddities." The third way was by way of scandal – sex, divorce, or police raids.

Monroe noted that she became a star through none of the above. Her fame was the result of sheer popularity, starting with the American soldiers fighting in the Korean War. Her legend somehow spread, and fan mail at the rate of 3,500 letters a week addressed to her arrived at the studio, eventually peaking at 7,000 letters a week – five times more mail than that received by Betty Grable, the studio's top star of the time. The 20th Century-Fox publicity folks were stumped, since no special campaign was ever marshalled on Monroe's behalf.

"The letters were pouring in only because moviegoers had seen me on the screen and felt excited enough to write or thank me or ask for my photograph," she wrote in *My Story*. "News that the public was hailing me as the new Hollywood movie favorite appeared in the Hollywood gossip columns. No one sent the news out. The columnists printed it because people were talking about it."

A thousand unusual things

Pretty Woman got people talking about Julia Roberts. It was Michelle's third film as a body double (only Kim Basinger and Catherine

Oxenberg had preceded Roberts), and it got the casting directors talked about Shelley Michelle.

But she was still a beautiful nobody. Because she never got credited.

Her first nude role was in *Rising Sun*, the Michael Crichton thriller, starring Sean Connery and Wesley Snipes. "I was credited as 'The Blonde,'" Michelle recalled. "I believe 20th Century-Fox interviewed a thousand girls for that role but Sean Connery had met me and he said, 'That's the girl I want to use!' I was like, 'Why?!!!' He's a leg man and he called me 'Legs.'" (Michelle repaid the compliment in her press interviews for the film. "I went on to say that I thought Scottish men were the sexiest.")

She also doubled for Madonna, in a 1994 television film called *Madonna: Innocence Lost*, based on the Madonna biography by Christopher Anderson. "The company had me double for Sandra Bullock and they said, 'Hey, do you want to do Madonna as well?' They called me back like the next day, and I said, 'Look, I'll do it for free!'"

Did she really? "No, they paid me," she laughed. "I said that because I've always thought of Madonna as my mentor. I've always admired her as businesswoman and for her talent. I'd met her at dance classes and clubs, though I didn't meet her to do this role. She was off doing *A League of Their Own* at the time, but it was done with her consent. It was one of the gigs I got because of *Pretty Woman*. I think by then, because I was the *Pretty Woman* body, everybody wanted me. So the minute she heard I was going to double her, she was like, 'Fine, perfect!'

"We reenacted a scene from a picture of her – she's sitting on her knees, topless, stroking a kitty cat. She shot me and then they shot her face off the book. They were doing the TV show around that book. I had the kitty cat on my lap, my knees curled underneath me, and I was stroking the kitty cat. They shot my whole body, front and back, and then superimposed her face. I think it was quite an honor to double for her – this was like playing the perfect body. She works out like crazy and she was in the best shape I'd ever seen."

"Being a body double has put me in all sorts of crazy situations," she sighed. "Things most people don't want to do. I've been put in freezing cold water and I had to take a blood bath. I was in *Bordello of Blood*, with (*Baywatch* star and *Playboy* Playmate) Erika Eleniak. There was a kind of sacrilegious part and she didn't want to do it. I've been called on for a thousand unusual things."

But is she then a thousand beautiful nobodies?

"You're there to do a sex scene and they think that's all you're here for," she noted. "I think there's a big misconception about body doubling. Body doubling is my job and I work with my body constantly, I think of camera angles, I think of how the actors react and I think of all the things that most normal people never think of. And they don't give you the credit. They think you're just this body, but there's a lot more to it that people just don't see."

So she does pay-per-view shows for *Playboy*, *Direct TV*, *In Demand,* and other cable outlets, all lucrative if somewhat marginalizing, but it gets her cutting-edge mindshare. "I currently have a library of over 40 shows. I feel it is rare to find an actress in the body-double and adult film world who can cross-over into the legitimate, mainstream acting world. I feel that the nudity taboo in Hollywood and the industry is completely changed, though, because of the Internet. It's like if you want to see nudity, go on the Internet, not to the movies."

In the summer of 2004, she was finally given the green light to attempt a starring role of her own, in a space action-hero series called *Galaxy Hunter*, to be shot in 2005. She won't be doubling for Tia Carrere in *Relic Hunter*, nor is it *Galaxy Quest*; Michelle's character, she explained merges Lara Croft with her persona, "Jane Blond DD7, a secret agent from Earth, but more campy." She has also been working on her third music CD, *My World*, and has launched her own wine label, Shelley Chardonnay, available on her website at US$12 a bottle.

But her most visible branding exercise, so to speak, has been in the fitness industry. She has endorsed the Joe Weider/Arnold Schwarzenegger "home gym" and appeared in the Gunthy/Renker "perfect buns machine" infomercial. And she launched, in November 2004, her own line of Body Double fitness products. ("The products are made with emu oil, which is natural healer for the joints and skin. We have 'sport sprays' for sore joints and muscles, and a whole line of beauty products as well.") Oil of Olay Body Wash previously hired her agency to test its product on 20 body-double actresses.

As an example of how people see her all the time but seldom know it, Michelle doubled for actress Suzanne Somers in her famous Thigh Master exercise machine infomercial. "They totally snuck me in behind her back, because they thought her hands look weathered," she recalled. "It's my hands and legs demonstrating the product, so it's my shape you're buying, not hers. She caught it a year later and made them pull it from the infomercial!"

Stardom is such an ephemeral thing, and sometimes one can forget that reaching for the stars is really a way of reaching for approval. Being a celebrity, after all, means losing some of yourself, to the deeply rooted projection of others, to mirror their own need for validation. This takes root in the creation of a fan culture, sometimes inspiring the kind of worship that one might not wish for.

"Yes, I am also 'Miss Armed Forces' for the USO, and I have weirdo fans who buy everything I have and can never seem to get enough," Michelle giggled. "They probably masturbate to my photos but usually compose themselves in front of me. I have been stalked a few times."

Ah, the perils of being a celebrity! If there's one thing she has learned in the past 12 years, it's surely this: The fans will think they have your body, so you should always keep your soul.

Eric Yeo

Eric Yeo is based in Kuala Lumpur, Malaysia, where he is a film critic and columnist for *Sin Chew Daily*, the country's largest-circulation, Chinese-language daily newspaper. He was previously the Managing Director of PolyGram Records Malaysia/Singapore, and considers himself a big fan of Elvis Presley, Cliff Richard and the Shadows, and the Beatles.

Have you ever bought anything because of a celebrity?

Yes, an Elvis T-shirt when I visited Graceland, and a Beatles T-shirt when I visited Liverpool, many years ago. But I also own something that might be worth quite a bit on *eBay*. I saw the Rolling Stones when they played in Singapore – in 1965! I still have my ticket. And I'm not selling it.

Why do you think Jackie Chan became the biggest Asian celebrity on a global scale?

Because action films appeal to a wider range of audience, and so they can easily transcend cultural differences and national barriers. He become the biggest Asian celebrity when *Rush Hour* made it big in the United States, but he is now trying very hard to make a comeback in Hong Kong films because his Hollywood career has almost come to an end. I think US audiences are finding him doing the same stunt over and over again, so they've become a bit fed up. His recent films *Tuxedo, The Medallion* and *Around The World in 80 Days* were box-office flops. I think his best hope is to score a big success in the China market.

What do you think of the popularity of Chinese movies in the West? Is this something that will last, if only because of Quentin Tarantino?

With or without Tarantino's name, it won't make that much of a difference, as far as I can see. I don't really think Chinese movies are very popular in the West. They are considered foreign-language, non-English films like the French, Italian, or German films, which also have had hits at some time or other. Ang Lee's *Crouching Tiger, Hidden Dragon* was good, but it was the Hollywood marketing machinery that helped push it to the maximum exposure level.

What do you think of the female stars like Zhang Ziyi, Michelle Yeoh and Maggie Cheung? Can their fame be "created" so that they can compete with Julia Roberts and Halle Berry?

The question is, will they be given meaty roles? They are all Chinese, and so film roles for them will be very limited. Michelle Yeoh's winning a Bond-girl role was like striking a lottery ticket. You have to accept the fact that the US film industry has their own "rules."

Even Halle Berry did not get any good scripts after *Monster's Ball*, and *Catwoman* was a joke.

What do you think of the way celebrities are made and marketed in Asia, in general? Is Asia behind the West in terms of how publicity works?

Marketing spend will have to be tailored according to market size, in order to be justifiable, especially with the China market opening up. I foresee that marketing and promotions for celebrities will be big in scale, though it's not fair to compare between the East and the West. The cultures, celebrity requirements, and the fans' acceptance levels are not the same. I think we still have a lot to learn from the West. They have been doing this way ahead of us for many years.

Can you share any insight into the fame and celebrity of the late Taiwanese singer Teresa Teng, since you were close to her?

She was a great singer, very charismatic, who never tried to follow the West. That made her very unique. Globally, all Chinese felt proud of her, because she was pure Chinese and not a Western copycat. There are not many Chinese artists about whom you could feel that way.

10
Tongues in Chic

On the evening of January 16, 2005, Leonardo DiCaprio ended his acceptance speech at the Golden Globe awards by appealing for people to continue contributing to the tsunami relief effort. He had just won the Best Actor award in the motion picture drama category for playing Howard Hughes in the new Martin Scorsese film, *The Aviator*, and donated US$1 million to UNICEF – a noteworthy gesture since he had once made a film on Phi Phi Island, off the coast of Thailand, now completely destroyed by the gigantic tidal wave quake of Boxing Day 2004.

The film, appropriately, was about backpackers traipsing through Thailand, many of whom in real life were now swept away into oblivion. DiCaprio and other Hollywood celebrities had garnered notices in many newspapers around the world for coming to the aid of the tsunami victims (most notably director Steven Spielberg, who donated US$1.5 million, and actress Sandra Bullock with US$1 million), though they were all upstaged by the Latino pop star Ricky Martin, who actually made a personal journey to Thailand (*USA Today*, on January 14, 2005, noted that Martin toured nearby Phuket Island "to meet with survivors and decide how his charity foundation can help them").

That was a nice touch, I thought, bringing into focus the role that celebrities can play in actually bringing a sense of mission into our lives, as opposed to being mere fodder for the tabloids (which, in that same week, were paying greater notice to the break-up of Brad Pitt and Jennifer Aniston). How interesting, I thought, that a natural disaster of such catastrophic scale would be a lynchpin for a new kind of celebrity tableaux, the kind that brings closer to home the real purpose they play in our lives.

The marketing pundits like to say that brands are becoming less and less about what we consume and more and more about who we are. Celebrity branding is, of course, the apex of this paradigm. And how strange indeed to note that this is a surreal juxtaposition of values, since only a mere six months prior to the tsunami, the celebrity of the year looked like it would undoubtedly be Paris Hilton.

I remembered all the hype, and wondered how long it would last. "Paris Hilton to be a brand name," was a line many newspapers adopted when reporting her media onslaught in the summer of 2004. Why? Well, she had a book out (*Confessions of an Heiress*) and a logo (a tiara with a "P" in the middle), to be used on new lines of lifestyle accessories: perfumes, cosmetics, eyewear, shoes, phone cards, compact discs, videos, and more. And all this after her reality television series *The Simple Life* had been certified a *bona fide* hit (with 10 million viewers on the American Fox network alone), a fact which spawned a deal with *Amazon.com* for "The Paris Hilton Collection," her very own jewelry line.

"There is no sin worse in life than being boring," the princess herself proclaimed in her 178-page book, certainly not a boring book at all since it was "more scrapbook than memoir, with pictures outnumbering paragraphs," as a Reuters story pointedly observed. It might be strange now to recall that most people had first heard of her only three years ago, thanks to an Internet-circulated home video of her having sex with a then-boyfriend.

I had last seen her onscreen in the film *Wonderland*, in which she played a party girl cozying up to Val Kilmer. The next thing anyone knew, she'd become a Guess? girl and her ads for the apparel company were suddenly everywhere. I actually liked how this treaded the fine line between elegance and decadence (or, as the more cynical would say, between good taste and bad). If pop culture icons as defined by mass-market acceptance are emblematic of our collective consciousness, then what have we now become? What is the future of pop culture in an age of idolatry born of mass-marketing prowess? More incisively, what can we really believe any more?

The goddess, our friend

A major point I've made throughout this book, however elliptical at times, is that fame is an idea that's less about people than about their "personalities." This is a critical difference, because "personalities" form the vital elements that embody the branding of a celebrity, though which our collective needs are then channeled. Many of us buy into this, and we would not have it any other way. For we are rewarded when these mirror images of ourselves stare, ever so handsomely, sometimes pensively, back at us.

It's an everlasting flame, because we are still witnessing the widespread dissemination of popular culture, largely the legacy of post-Second World War United States hegemony. America, as the predominant world economy, imprinted its lifestyle on the rest of the world. The growth of suburbia led to the growth of the multiple-screen cineplexes, and the advent of FM radio allowed for hours and hours of drive-time programming as cars took to the freeways. There's satellite television and the propensity of limitless cable programming, and by 2005, things had reached a new peak with the ubiquity of the iPod.

Why anyone would need 3,000 songs in a compact, hand-held, 15-gigabyte device (already rendered obsolete by newer 40-gigabyte models) is no longer the point. The availability of alternatives, and a surfeit of consumer choices, has become a given. As Michael J. Wolf, the founder of the Media and Entertainment Group at the consulting giant Booz-Allen & Hamilton, noted: "Locally, globally, internationally, we are living in an entertainment economy."

One of the things I liked about his 1999 book, *The Entertainment Economy: How mega-media forces are transforming our lives*, was the example of how the commercial airline industry was seduced by the power of entertainment. After surveys showed that airline passengers spent 40 percent of their time in the air using in-flight entertainment and 35 percent sleeping, major carriers like Virgin Atlantic and Singapore Airlines began installing state-of-the-art in-flight entertainment systems – whereby one can watch, via video screens on every seat, a wide choice of movies and play a variety of computer games, as well as access the old-hat audio channels. Since many first-run movies are now available in-flight, the immediacy of this cross-pollination of pop iconography is nothing short of awesome. With 22 in-flight movies to choose from, who needs Nintendo?

In our heads, we are parsing this awesome collusion of information, much of which feeds our subconscious impulses. What did it matter to anyone that *Forbes* magazine in 2002 ranked Julia Roberts number 26 on its annual list of the 40 richest people in America under the age of 40? Nothing, except that Julia Roberts was estimated to have a net worth of US$145 million. Marilyn Monroe may have said, "I don't care about money, I just want to be wonderful," in part a mocking gesture to her gross underpayment by the Hollywood studio system of her time, but now we want to embrace a screen queen who can be both wonderful and rich. Too many people are wonderful already anyway.

Julia Roberts's appeal, in point of fact, was brilliant dissected by the *New Yorker* film critic Anthony Lane: "The essence of Roberts's appeal – notably old-fashioned, if you think about it – is that she is more lovable than desirable, and that, even when love is off the menu, she cannot not be liked. There is no more flattering illusion in movies, none that we prefer to hear over and over again: here is a goddess, and she wants to be your friend."

I think it's important to note that Roberts became a star because of a very successful film called *Pretty Woman*, in which she played a prostitute in Beverly Hills. That, alone, may have initiated the entire cycle, whereby the masses at large have given tacit approval to the female sexual being as cultural icon (even if no one can ever imagine Paris Hilton or Jenna Jameson in the very same role, with or without Richard Gere). Somewhere along the line, that idea became socially acceptable in part because of the sheer visibility of certain celebrities.

Photographs in daily newspapers everywhere verify this. Roberts was seen traveling to Haiti to view the plight of refugees in 1996, when she was a UNICEF Goodwill Ambassador. Singer Geri Halliwell, formerly of the Spice Girls, did the same in 1998, traveling to the Philippines that year as the Goodwill Ambassador for the United Nations Population Fund. The latest in this line of highly effective, goody-two-shoes politicking involved the unflappable, unstoppable Angelina Jolie, who, as a Goodwill Ambassador for UNHCR (the United Nations High Commission on Refugees), even wrote a book about it (the coyly titled *Notes from My Travels*, published in October 2003).

Jolie personified rectitude by example – she adopted a Cambodian son, bought a house in Cambodia, and donated large sums of money to the country. None of this would have been possible without her role as Lara Croft in *Tomb Raider*, the project that sent her there in the first place and opened her eyes to the Third World. One can infer that it was Jolie's way of "paying back" for the good fortune of being a movie star. (She even spent Christmas 2004 in, of all places, Beirut!)

The celebrity who'd started this charity ball rolling was Audrey Hepburn, the United Nations Goodwill Ambassador for UNICEF in 1987. She had visited places as far-flung as Bangladesh, Ethiopia, Sudan, and Vietnam, but was diagnosed with colon cancer after returning from Somalia in 1991, and finally died in 1993. Hepburn had gained fame as the sassy call-girl Holly Golightly in *Breakfast at Tiffany's* (though others might remember her more as the more prim if similarly headstrong Eliza Doolittle in *My Fair Lady*). At any rate, some people at the United Nations clearly knew that attention would be paid.

The legacy of possibilities

When I began researching for this project, I read branding consultant Wally Olins's book *On Brand*, in which he stated: "What marketing, branding and all the rest of it are about is persuading, seducing and attempting to manipulate people into buying products and services.... Branding these days is largely about involvement and association; the outward and visible demonstration of private and personal affiliation. Branding enables us to define ourselves in terms of a shorthand that is immediately comprehensible to the world around us."

"The brand is ideally suited to the age of the soundbite and the global village," Olins added. "It says a huge amount to like-minded people, wherever they live, all in one go.... Brands represent clarity, reassurance, consistency, status, membership – everything that enables human beings to help define themselves. Brands represent identity."

We see this in the pop music world, in the Bee Gees and Abba and the Pet Shop Boys – all entities associated with a certain kitsch appeal. Of course, catchy hooks and hummable melodies help; who knows how many young Americans were lured to visit London because of the Pet Shop Boys' best-known song, "West End Girls"? Ultimately, that's what our celebrities do for us: they offer reassurance and give voice to amorphous, nameless notions swirling around in our heads – those that reassure us that we are not alone in aspiring to be the kind of people we want to be.

Why else would a naïve but ambitious brunette named Norma Jean Baker peroxide herself in the manner of blondes that came before, like Jayne Mansfield and Mae West? To be pretty and blonde was considered desirable, but to be pretty and blonde on a 40-foot silver screen for the viewing pleasure of millions was surely the finest validation of all. You too, she implied by her example, can also be larger than life.

In a special theme issue of *L.A. Style* magazine ("Hollywood: Legends and Legacies," December 1986), its executive editor and my mentor, the late Bob LaBrasca, wrote about this very matter:

> We're jaded. How could we not be? This is the Age of Narcissism in the city that fantasy built and which, in return, has fed the fantasies of untold millions. This is the end of the Yellow Brick Road, where it really is all done with lights and mirrors. Now and again, we locals sneak a peek behind the arras and into the vacant eyes of the funny little man who pulls the levers and flips the switches, and we come away a little bit more disillusioned but all the more fascinated with the gimmickry that makes the magic work.... And that's perhaps Hollywood's truest legacy – the legacy of possibilities.

People who worship celebrities are people who believe in possibilities, and to varying extents we all do. How many young girls have already vowed to becomes actresses because they saw Natalie Portman win a Golden Globe in January 2005 (with Meryl Streep competing in the same category?!!) or liken herself to the way Claire Danes "walks that fine line between the naiveté of youth and the passion of someone much wiser than her age would allow" (as I had observed in a film review I once wrote of Baz Luhrmann's *Romeo + Juliet*). As many marketers who have studied MTV have surely observed, youth and passion are the very touchstones of popular culture, and so it's worth looking at the key ingredients that make them viable commodities.

The passion of the young is not to be easily dismissed, as baby boomers themselves learned when they themselves were targeted for the libertarian ideals they'd embraced back in the 1960s and 1970s; how else can one explain the existence of television shows like *The West Wing* and even *Sex and the City*? It's also interesting to note how this was happening almost exactly 40 years since the Beatles first landed in America and changed the cultural landscape forever, in part inducting people into newer realms of social and sexual mores. They also incited the kind of fan fever that would be repeated over and over again, in countless forms and guises.

That's what was really happening in January 2005 when the red vinyl dress worn by singer Gwen Stefani on the cover of *Tragic Kingdom*, the 1995 hit debut album of her band No Doubt, was stolen from a museum in Southern California. The US$5,000 dress was on display in an exhibit devoted to the history of rock music in the band's hometown area, Orange County (a place television viewers elsewhere now know because of the hit show, *The O.C.*). Since *Tragic Kingdom* sold 15 million copies worldwide, any number of people could have perpetrated the theft – not to mention many more closet kleptomaniacs who must have fantasized about it. But what could possibly drive someone to do such a thing?

Perhaps it's the same motive that drives someone to visit the "Hollywood Forever" cemetery in Los Angeles, where people can visit the graves of hundreds of stars like Rudolph Valentino, Cecil B. DeMille and even Mel Blanc (the voice of Bugs Bunny). Call it the insatiable need to view or possess something that was once part of one's own psychological make-up. Nostalgia is an intangible, ineffable thing that can be translated into dollars at the cash register, hence the existence of so many music and movie memorabilia stores. When the Internet took over in the mid-1990s it prompted the bricks-and-mortar to become the clicks-and-mortar, with many of these places migrating to online sales for better, quicker revenue gain. This is but only one example of the way our devotion to our favorite celebrities can lead to spiritual exaltation, the kind that some say has now replaced religion.

War of the worlds

Well, why not? In earlier chapters on this book, I've pointed to instances of how celebrity worship has become an idol worship, often more fervent and rabid than any church service. It doesn't help when people surf the Internet for movie star news and read, for instance, about how Tom Cruise has signed a deal that will make him the highest-earning actor ever – he is expected to earn a staggering US$360 million for his role in the Steven Spielberg film *War of the Worlds*. According to the Internet Movie Database website (imdb.com), Cruise's unique deal gives him not a set fee for his role but rather 10 percent of the film's box-office earnings plus profit-sharing from DVDs, video games, and toys. The film itself is projected to make at least US$1.8 billion, of which Cruise will take US$180 million, and then there are the two planned sequels which should double that.

At the time of writing, the film hasn't been finished. But that's not the point. The point is, what would people see in Tom Cruise that could make him such a hugely bankable star? Hollywood films require expansive outlays of investment money, and deals like that don't come easily without some kind of justification for massive above-the-line costs. But some film financiers who will look at words like "Spielberg" and "Cruise" and, without hesitation, commit their checkbooks. That's where the rubber has met the road, because they know that moviegoers will flock to the theatres, drawn in droves over the sight of their favorite celebrity names on the marquee.

However, what has also happened is that the pop culture world has somehow managed to knowledge-transfer its infectious, quirky charms. Companies that are not even in the entertainment arena now hire "buzz creators" (as some major hotels have done for the past few years) to launch new properties and products. "Youth marketing" has become a known industry, though it brings to my mind something that David Bowie once said: "There's not much outrageousness left any more.... The Beatles were outrageous at one time, and so was Mick Jagger, but can't remain at the top for five years and still be outrageous.... You become accepted and the impact has gone."

Writer Barney Hoskyns was quoting Bowie there, in a 2002 career retrospective piece in Britain's *Independent*. The kicker is this: The quote itself was something Bowie had said a whole 30 years earlier, back in 1972! This is the real war of the worlds, because fame moves in cycles and seasons, and everything old is then somehow new again. Yet this is my best hope for the future of celebrity branding. There will always be another Britney Spears beating Kylie Minogue in the American market, another Jennifer Lopez leveraging on sex appeal to sell perfumes and clothes, another Bruce Lee or Jackie Chan to elevate the cultural status of the action hero.

But without the real replenishment of true talent and the bold resurgence of artistic nerve, all we would be getting would be more cookie-cutter effluvium, more contrived clutter being recycled to the awestruck masses.

Witness, for example, the current success of rock bands like Jet, a veritable godsend to kids today who missed out on Aerosmith in their heyday. To my mind, that's almost the same as say, the way young Ashlee Simpson is milking the pop-punk aesthetic to sell more records than her teen-pop diva sister Jessica, though it will be interesting indeed to see if either of them will be around in five years. The difference is slight, because it's always about embracing the new with a constant challenge – to separate the flotsam and jetsam from the good idols who become great icons. That's the underlying reason why so many "pop idol" contests are suddenly the rage the world over.

We revel in the sudden success of these amateur singers because we are subconsciously trying to celebrate some part of ourselves yearning for validation, even if for one brief shining moment, and even as we know fame to be fleeting and mass adulation a falsehood based on delusion. With every gap-toothed nod to blind aspiration, William Hung lives on. Enough people want him to reflect their own tone-deaf earnestness.

However, even as I blanch at this kind of gauche phenomenon, I know too that this is what brought me to pop culture in the first place. There is a sort of middlebrow curiosity I have for it, which keeps me interested and engaged. Naturally, hero worship can be both wonderful and deadly (or else Mark Chapman wouldn't still be in jail for killing John Lennon), but I know that it also informs the very core of some of our lives, that deep-set part of our psyches where wonderment lies beyond words yet can be conjured into existence by certain sights, certain sounds, even certain smells and other sensual textures. The branding of a celebrity is actually a way of tapping into the human condition, of accessing our ambitions, even if vicarious pleasure always exacts a price.

Even those of us who know all this are willing to pay for the ride, simply because we crave the journey. It's not always a bad thing to want, though one has keep the tongue in chic, as I like to say, because you never know what you can learn from anything. Yesterday's heroes can become tomorrow's fools, depending on our attention span, but I like to think that we all need to cling to our memories. The value of our pop culture icons lies in the way they often remind us of the people we want to become. For that reason alone they will be with us, and will never go away.

REFERENCES AND SUGGESTED READING

Several books served as research sources for this book, and the following are recommended for further reading:

Berger, John. *Ways of Seeing*. London: BBC/Penguin, 1972.

Boyd, Jenny (with George-Warren, Holly). *Musicians In Tune: Seventy-five contemporary musicians discuss the creative process*. New York: Fireside, 1992.

Bystedt, Karen Hardy. *Before They Were Famous: In their own words*. Santa Monica: General Publishing Group, 1996.

Chan, Jackie (with Yang, Jeff). *I Am Jackie Chan: My life in action*. New York: Ballantine, 1998.

Chow, Rey. *Primitive Passions: Visuality, sexuality, ethnography, and contemporary Chinese cinema*. New York: Columbia University Press, 1995.

Clifton, Rita, Simmons, John, et al. *Brands and Branding*. London: Profile, 2003.

Coleridge, Nicholas. *The Fashion Conspiracy: A remarkable journey through the empires of fashion*. New York: Harper & Row, 1988.

Coupland, Douglas. *Polaroids From the Dead*. New York: Regan Books, 1997.

Fisher, Carrie. *Postcards From the Edge*. New York: Simon & Schuster, 1987.

George, Nelson. *Hip Hop America*. New York: Viking, 1998.

Gladwell, Malcolm. *The Tipping Point: How little things can make a big difference*. London: Abacus, 2001.

Gross, Michael. *Model: The ugly business of beautiful women.* New York: William Morrow, 1995.

Guiles, Fred Lawrence. *Jane Fonda: The actress in her time.* London: Michael Joseph, 1981.

Hammond, Stefan and Wilkins, Mike. *Sex and Zen and a Bullet in the Head: The essential guide to Hong Kong's mind-bending films.* New York: Fireside, 1996

Heard, Christopher. *Ten Thousand Bullets: The cinematic journey of John Woo.* Los Angeles: Lone Eagle, 2000.

Hoskyns, Barney (ed.). *The Sound and the Fury: 40 years of classic rock journalism: A Rock's Backpages reader.* London: Bloomsbury, 2003.

Loder, Kurt. *Bat Chain Puller: Rock & roll in the age of celebrity.* New York: St Martin's Press, 1990.

Marcus, Greil. *Double Trouble: Bill Clinton and Elvis Presley in a land of no alternatives.* New York: Picador, 2000.

McCann, Graham. *Marilyn Monroe: The body in the library.* Cambridge: Polity Press, 1988.

Monroe, Marilyn. *My story.* New York, Stein and Day, 1976.

Newton, Helmut. *Autobiography.* New York: Nan A. Talese, 2003.

Olins, Wally, *On Brand.* London: Thames & Hudson, 2003.

Pringle, Hamish. *Celebrity Sells.* Chichester: John Wiley, 2004.

Puttnam, David (with Watson, Neil). *The Undeclared War: The struggle for control of the world's film industry.* London: Harper-Collins, 1997.

Raphael, Jordan and Spurgeon, Tom. *Stan Lee and the Rise and Fall of the American Comic Book.* Chicago: Chicago Review Press, 2003.

Spada, James. *Julia: Her life.* New York: St Martin's Press, 2004.

Wolf, Michael J. *The Entertainment Economy: How mega-forces are transforming our lives*. London: Penguin, 2000.

Additional references

The following are also referenced in the text, or were used as reference sources in writing it:

Anderson, Pamela. *Star: A novel*. New York: Atria, 2004.

Batey, Ian. *Asian Branding: A great way to fly*. London: Pearson Education Asia, 2002.

Benson, Michael. *Gloria Estefan*. Minneapolis: Lerner Publications, 2000.

Blackett, Tom. "What is a brand," in *Brands and Branding*, London: Economist/Profile, 2003.

Bockris, Victor. *Warhol: The biography*. New York: De Capo Press, 2003.

Booker, Christopher. *The Neophiliacs: The revolution in English life in the Fifties and Sixties*. London: Collins, 1969.

Campbell, Naomi. *Swan*. London: Heinemann, 1994.

Clark, Paul. *Chinese Cinema: Culture and Politics Since 1949*. Cambridge: Cambridge University Press, 1987.

Fleming, Charles. *High Concept: Don Simpson and the Hollywood Culture of Excess*. New York: Doubleday, 1998.

Ford, Tom. *Tom Ford*. New York: Rizzoli, 2004.

Haber, Karen (ed.). *Exploring the Matrix: Visions of a cyber future*. New York: St Martin's Press, 2003.

Hackett, Pat (ed.). *The Andy Warhol Diaries*. London: Simon & Schuster, 1989.

Heinlein, Robert. *Stranger in a Strange Land.* London: New English Library, 1992.

Helvin, Marie. *Catwalk: The art of model style.* London: Pavilion/ Michael Joseph, 1985.

Hilton, Paris and Ginsberg, Merle. *Confessions of an Heiress: A tongue-in-chic peek behind the pose.* London: Simon & Schuster, 2004.

Jolie, Angelina. *Notes from My Travels: Visits with refugees in Africa, Cambodia, Pakistan and Ecuador.* New York: Simon & Schuster, 2003.

King, Tom. *The Operator: David Geffen builds, buys and sells the new Hollywood.* New York: Random House, 2000.

Klein, Naomi. *No Logo.* London: Flamingo, 2001.

Kramer, Peter. *Listening to Prozac: A psychiatrist explores antidepressant drugs and the remaking of the self.* London: Fourth Estate, 1994.

Lords, Traci Elizabeth. *Traci Lords: Underneath it all.* New York: Harper Entertainment/HarperCollins, 2003.

Mathis, Carla and Connor, Helen Villa. *The Triumph of Individual Style: A guide to dressing your body, your beauty, your self.* Menlo Park, Calif.: Timeless Editions, 1994.

McCarthy, Jenny. *Jen-X: Jenny McCarthy's open book.* London: HarperCollins, 1997.

Minogue, Kylie and Baker, William. *Kylie: La La La.* London: Hodder & Stoughton, 2003.

Newton, Helmut. *White Women.* London: Quartet, 1979.

Packard, Vance. *The Hidden Persuaders.* London: Penguin Books, 1970.

Reinstein, Mara and Bartolomeo, Joey. *Brad and Jen: The rise and fall of Hollywood's golden couple.* New York: Wenner Books, 2005.

Ries, Al and Ries, Laura. *The 11 Immutable Laws of Internet Branding.* London: HarperCollins, 2000.

Spade, Kate. *Manners.* London: Simon & Schuster, 2004.

Spade, Kate. *Occasions.* London: Simon & Schuster, 2004.

Spade, Kate. *Style.* London: Simon & Schuster, 2004.

Stanley-Clarke, Jenny. *Kylie Naked: A biography.* London: Ebury Press, 2002.

Tangye, Dave and Wright, Graham. *How Black was our Sabbath.* London: Sidgwick and Jackson, 2004.

Taschen's Photobooks. *Madonna Nudes 1979.* New York: Taschen, 1992.

Turner, Steve. "How to Become a Cult Figure in Only Two Years: The Making of David Bowie," in Barney Hoskyns (ed.), *The Sound and the Fury: 40 years of classic rock journalism: A Rock's Backpages reader.* London: Bloomsbury, 2003.

Twitchell, James. *Lead Us into Temptation: The triumph of American materialism.* New York: Columbia University Press, 1999.

Wilde, Oscar. *Phrases and Philosophies for the Use of the Young.* Oxford: The Chameleon, 1894.

Yule, Andrew. *Fast Fade: David Puttnam, Columbia Pictures and the battle for Hollywood.* New York: Doubleday, 1989.

INDEX

213